ACTIVE WRITERS

YEAR 4

Eileen Jones

Hopscotch

A division of MA Education Ltd

Hopscotch

A division of MA Education Ltd

Published by Hopscotch, a division of
MA Education, St Jude's Church,
Dulwich Road, London, SE24 0PB
www.hopscotchbooks.com
020 7738 5454

©2013 MA Education Ltd

Written by Eileen Jones

Series designed by Claire White,
Fonthill Creative, 01722 717029

Illustrated by Kerry Bailey

Associate Publisher: Angela Morano Shaw

ISBN 978-1-907515-69-9

Every effort has been made to trace the owners of copyright of material in this book and the publisher apologises for any inadvertent omissions. Any persons claiming copyright for any material should contact the publisher who will be happy to pay the permission fees agreed between them and who will amend the information in this book on any subsequent reprint.

Charlotte's Web by E B White (Hamish Hamilton, 1952) Copyright © 1952 by J White.

"Conversation" by Michael Rosen from *Wouldn't you like to know* (© Michael Rosen, 1977) is printed by permission of United Agents (www.unitedagents.co.uk) on behalf of Michael Rosen.

Contents

INTRODUCTION

About the series

Active Writers is a new and exciting literacy series, which aims to provide children with the tools to become more competent and confident writers.

This is done by using a structured approach, thus inviting learners to:

- Review what they know about a text genre

- Learn about the writing devices used

- Practise the language skills needed

- Apply their learning in a writing task.

Active Writers expects greater independence of thought. It includes resources to ensure children can assess their own progress in collaboration with their teacher and therefore:

- Self-Assessment is required

- Teacher-pupil discussion is prompted

- Teacher assessment is catered for

- A signed record is produced.

There are 5 books with CDs in the **Active Writers** series:

- Year 2 (Ages 6-7)

- Year 3 (Ages 7-8)

- Year 4 (Ages 8-9)

- Year 5 (Ages 9-10)

- Year 6 (Ages 10-11)

Each book is divided into three broad text categories:

- Narrative

- Non-fiction

- Poetry.

There are 12 fully-planned lessons, each accompanied by an exemplar text in a different genre. Many of these texts are original extracts from well known authors, with 6 lesson plans for Narrative, 4 for Non-fiction and 2 for Poetry. The lesson explores the writing style and key features of the exemplar text and provides class, partner and independent work support.

The language skills needed for the text type are identified, explained and practised in the activities on the two 'Practice in Writing Skills' sheets. Differentiation is also catered for.

Children are then ready for the writing task.

Guide notes are provided together with differentiated help and a writing framework supplied for less confident writers.

At the end of the task, children will assess their finished piece. The self-assessment sheet itemises the features the children should have included. The clear tick-box format helps the children to identify what they might have overlooked and will ask to include written comments about what they might do to improve their next writing in this genre.

The same sheet leaves space for the teacher's comments and also asks both children and teacher to 'sign' confirmation that they have discussed the writing features.

About this book

This book is for **Year 4** children.

Lesson plan
Use the lesson as early work. Begin by asking the children to define the genre. Return to the definition in later weeks. Ask the children if they need to amend their definition.

Exemplar text
An exemplar text is supplied with each lesson plan. Texts will cover a variety of genres to give children experience of a wide range of texts.

Writing skills practice
Use the practice pages for emphasis on the writing skills identified in the exemplar text. Most of the class should complete Sections A and B; less able children will do Section A only; the most able will progress to the end of the page. In general class reading, point out examples of the writing devices.

Writing task
This is the culmination of the lesson: children applying what they have learned in their writing feature. Encourage the children to use the guide to plan and do initial drafts, before their final editing results in a polished version.

Self-assessment sheet
Encourage the children to think carefully about their answers and comments. Make sure your discussion with the children

over their writing is meaningful, offering positive advice about where they can improve and asking them to view the signatures as important evidence of their work. Keep the sheet as filed evidence of the learner's progress.

- The exemplar texts

- Answers and additional resources.

Using the CD

Each book includes a CD for easy use on the Interactive Whiteboard. The CD contains:

- A differentiated writing frame for a lower level of ability

Sample lesson plan

Title of the text
Genre and definition
Lesson objective This indicates the focus of the lesson and is a reminder of the need to view the text as a writer.

Warm up activity	Features
This part should be done first, with the purpose of orientating the children with the exemplar text, its genre and some key writing characteristics.	This is a reference tool. It guides the teacher, provides answers, and can be displayed as a reference for the children during 'Independent writing'.
Writing investigation **Ask the children:** This part is addressed to the children. It frequently encourages partner discussion and written recording as the children examine the text's style and writing techniques.	**Independent writing** **Ask the children:** This is the main part of the lesson. It involves further examination of the exemplar text – for example, how the writer has sketched characters – and asks for similar writing from the children.

Differentiation
This part provides extension and support work for children with those needs. It links to tasks in 'Independent writing'.

Plenary
This offers opportunities for self and peer assessment of the independent writing and reinforces understanding of the writing features.

The London Children

Narrative: Stories with historical settings

Definition: *"A story about the past."*

Lesson objective
To plan and write a story set in the past.

Warm up activity

- Display and read aloud the exemplar text.

- Ask: *What type of narrative is this?*
  Let partners exchange answers before you accept an answer. Identify it as a story with a historical setting.

- Let partners confer on the time period, suggesting a year in which the text was set. Ask them to hold up their whiteboards with a year. Agree on Victorian times

- Circle *maze* in the final sentence.
  Suggest that it is used literally and figuratively: people lose their way in these streets; Albert and Nancy could become trapped in danger.

Features

Setting of a previous time period

Realistic characters

Places or things from that time

Powerful verbs

What to look out for

Character differences from the present day: speech, dress or behaviour

Past tense

Descriptive detail about the setting

Writing investigation
Ask the children:

- Reread the text. Talk to your partner about your reaction to the street children. Identify two words or facts that present them as 'good' characters. (They are orphans; the way people treat them; *pleaded, trustingly, starving*.)

- Talk to your partner about Dogsworth. Does he intend good or harm to the children? Identify two words that make the reader react unfavourably to him. (*Scowling, oozed, sneered, sneaked*.)

- Identify and list three details that confirm the text's historical setting. (Muffs, carriages, top hats, farthing.)

Independent writing
Ask the children:

- Share ideas with a partner about what will happen to Albert and Nancy. Will Dogsworth get them jobs? What?

- Reread the final, one-line paragraph. Are you confident about Albert and Nancy's safety? Write a few notes about what could happen next. Use the notes to tell your story orally to a partner.

- With a partner, find out about working Victorian children. You can use this Internet website: www.bbc.co.uk/schools/primaryhistory/victorian_britain
  Make notes about jobs and working conditions.

Differentiation
- More confident writers find out about the law bringing in a working age of 10 years.
- Less confident writers note just three facts about working Victorian children.

Plenary

Talk about Dr Barnardo. Use the internet website http://www.bbc.co.uk/schoolradio/subjects/history/victorians/chimneysweep/barnardo for the children to listen to accounts of Barnardo's rescue of children, such as Albert and Nancy.

The London Children

"Spare us a farthing! Give us a farthing!" pleaded a child's voice.
It was bitterly cold, an icy wind was blowing and snow was starting to settle on the cobbled London street. Ladies nestled their hands into their muffs and walked carefully towards waiting carriages. Gentleman pushed their top hats more firmly on to their hands and strode purposefully about their business. Most of them ignored the two bare-footed children in rags who stood at the side of the street.

A richly-dressed lady hesitated a moment, but her companion urged her on. "Keep away from him," she said. "These London street children are filthy. Look at the dirt on his feet."
Albert and his younger sister, Nancy, had been begging all day. Now snow would make their job even harder. Still they had to keep trying: they had eaten nothing since yesterday.

"A crust of bread, sir!" called Nancy and stretched out her hands towards a wealthy-looking gentleman.
"Just a farthing! Only a farthing!" pleaded Harry.
"Be off!" bellowed the gentleman and brandished his walking stick at the children.
"What's all this then?" growled a scowling man who had sneaked up behind the children.
"We're starving, sir," said Harry.
"Our parents are dead. We need food."
"Oh dear, all alone in the world are you?" oozed the grim stranger.
The children nodded.
"You know what you need, don't you? A job!" sneered the man.
"But we're only nine and eight. We're too young," said Harry.
"Rubbish! My name's Dogsworth and I'm a man who knows what's what. No one's too young for work! You come along with Dogsworth. I'll give you a nice place to work and stay."

Trustingly, the children followed Dogsworth into the maze of London's narrow streets.

Practice in Writing Skills 1

| Powerful verbs | A powerful verb gives extra meaning to a sentence by describing character, mood and atmosphere. The boy learning to swim _clutched_ the rubber ring. |

Section A

Find the powerful verbs in the story text.

The first one has been completed for you.

b e g g e d

pl _ _ _ _ _

se _ _ _ _

st _ _ _ _

ne _ _ _ _ _

be _ _ _ _ _ _

gr _ _ _ _ _

u _ _ _ _

br _ _ _ _ _ _ _ _

sn _ _ _ _ _

o _ _ _ _

br _ _ _ _ _ _ _

Use a verb in the box to replace the verb underlined in each sentence, changing the tense if needed. Cross out any other words no longer needed. The first one has been done.

The man really _frightened_ the street children. ➔

The man ~~really~~ _terrified_ the street children.

frown	loathe	growl
glare	shove	trudge
snatch	~~terrify~~	glower
shriek	threaten	

He <u>looked</u> angrily at Nancy.

He <u>made</u> threats to Albert.

He <u>pushed</u> the boy roughly into the room.

He <u>took</u> away quickly the money they were given.

Section B

Think of 10 powerful verbs instead of these. The first one has been done.

asked in a begging voice   **pleaded** _____

gave a big smile _____

got better _____

made a moaning sound _____

spoke unpleasantly _____

looked at with open mouth _____

laughed sarcastically _____

looked very angry _____

said firmly _____

Practice in Writing Skills 2

Effective description → Adjectives (single words) and adjectival phrases describe a place, person or thing.
They improve the visual image given to the reader.

Section A

Five sentences contain an adjective; the last three sentences contain an adjectival phrase. Underline them. Circle the nouns or pronouns they describe. The first one is done for you.

Harry and Alice were very *poor* children.

A kind stranger had rescued them from London.
He asked his housekeeper to find spare clothes.
The housekeeper was unhappy but she agreed.
The children were safe.
However, the man was hatching a mysterious plot.
The house was quite big.
The owner must have been quite rich.

Adjectives and adjectival phrases can have the same meaning. Draw lines to pair these.

adjectives	adjectival phrases
swift	quite dear
glum	exactly the same
terrified	absolutely sure
irritable	very, very fast
certain	rather miserable
identical	extremely frightened
costly	a bit cross

Section B

Fill the gaps with adjectives and adjectival phrases from the box.

Harry was given the _____ job
of chimney sweep's boy. He had to work _____
hours, so the job was _____ . He often
went to _____ houses that
had _____ chimneys. The chimneys
had some _____ parts. Harry had to
squeeze through _____ gaps. He had
to push the _____ .

adjectives	adjectival phrases
long	really unsafe
cleaning	very tall
grand	very scared
tight	very tiring
thick	
narrow	
dangerous	

Independent writing task

Continue the story of Albert and Nancy as they are forced to work. Use this guide to help you plan.

1. The place where the children work Choose an unpleasant place where the children are together.	**2. My new characters** Name two or three characters that the children work for or with.
3. How I want readers to react to my characters Decide whether you want the reader to see your characters as 'good' or 'bad'.	**4. Other characters** Let Dogsworth still appear in the story.
5. Historical details to remind readers of the time period Mention three or four things from Victorian times.	**6. What happened** Write notes or phrases about what happened as the children worked. Were they treated badly? Did one good person befriend them?
7. Powerful verbs for my characters' actions Use verbs that describe the characters' personalities. Use the past tense.	**8. My final sentence** Stop at an interesting moment. Include a word that will make the reader wonder about further danger.

Self-assessment

Read the story you wrote. How well did you do?
Tick the features you can see in it.

Name: _____ Date: _____

- ☐ I have set my story in a previous time period.
- ☐ I have added descriptive detail to my setting.
- ☐ I mention places and things from the past.
- ☐ My characters are realistic.
- ☐ My characters differ from today in speech, dress or behaviour.
- ☐ I have used some powerful verbs.
- ☐ My story is in the past tense.

Next time, I would improve my story by ...

Teacher's comment

I have talked to my teacher about my work on stories with historical settings.

Pupil: _____

Teacher: _____

The Loft Dwellers

Narrative: Stories set in imaginary worlds

Definition: *"A story that is set in a fantasy world."*

Lesson objective
To explain how writers use figurative and expressive language to create mental images and atmosphere.

Warm up activity
- Display and read aloud the exemplar text as far as '*... a voice on his right*. Underline the early sentence *This ... loft*. Ask: *What atmosphere is immediately established?* (Unreal.)

- Ask: *What type of narrative does this extract seem to be?* Let partners exchange answers before you accept answers from the class. Conclude that it is a story set in an imaginary world.

- Finish reading the text aloud.

Features

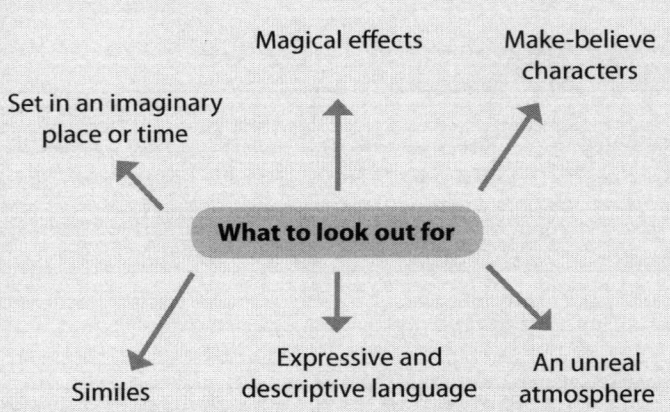

Magical effects
Make-believe characters
Set in an imaginary place or time
What to look out for
Similes
Expressive and descriptive language
An unreal atmosphere

Writing investigation
Ask the children:

- Reread the text. Discuss the characters with your partner. Identify three ways in which they seem imaginary. What magical effect is described in the story? (Food comes to you when pointed to.)

- Read aloud the paragraph about the food while your partner draws what they 'see'. Exchange roles and afterwards compare pictures.

- Investigate the expressive adjectives, phrases or imagery responsible for giving more details of your pictures. (*splendid, bulky, rainbow-coloured*.) Identify two unusual comparisons. (*Jellies like volcanoes; marshmallows like pillows*.) What are these unusual comparisons called? (Similes.)

Independent writing
Ask the children:

- Imagine the next part of the story. What did Josh see as he looked around? How was it strange and unreal? Share ideas with a partner and write the objects you will describe.

- Write some expressive adjectives or phrases to use, and an interesting comparison in a simile.

- Write the next two paragraphs of the story. Keep the mood of fantasy and make the paragraphs connect well.

Differentiation
- More confident writers may write at greater length with details of a character or happening.
- Less confident writers work with a partner and write one paragraph.

Plenary
Form small reading groups, the children reading their story extensions to one another. Encourage constructive feedback about the worlds imagined.

The Loft Dwellers

This was not an ordinary loft. A long table with a brightly-coloured tablecloth was set with food. Busy eaters sat on both sides of the table, cross-legged, without chairs or benches, but actually on the table.

"Sit – down! Sit – down!" ordered a voice, in a clear, robotic tone.
Josh tried to obey, but first he had to climb on to the table and find a place. He was expecting the firm surface of the tables he knew. He certainly did not expect one that bucked and swayed beneath his feet. With every movement, a cup of tea went over, a cake flew into the air, or a sandwich struck his face. There were howls of protest from all sides.

"You're – not – like – us," said a voice on his right.
That was true. For a start, they were green! Their round heads were too large for their short bodies. They had prominent eyes that seemed to stand out on stalks, stared fiercely, and swivelled suddenly in new directions. But it was their arms and legs that were most noticeable. They were too long, too spindly, and too... numerous. There were just too many limbs! It was difficult to be sure, but Josh thought they had six each. In fact, with some of the diners he thought he counted eight.

Once seated, Josh took in the contents of the table. Admittedly, his footprints had spoilt many things but it was still a splendid spread: mountains of bulky sandwiches, purple and yellow jellies like spurting volcanoes, rainbow-coloured cakes of every shape, and white dimpled marshmallows like pillows.
"What- do – you – want – to – eat?" asked a voice opposite.
"I'd like one of those, please," said Josh politely, and pointed to the highest peak.
A sandwich flew obediently into his outstretched hand.
As Josh munched, he looked around the room.

Practice in Writing Skills 1

Interesting comparisons

A comparison relates one thing to another.
Interesting comparisons create strong visual images.

Section A

Use joining lines to compare the nine nouns in Column A to those in Column B.

The first one is done for you.

Column A	Column B
chair	claw
white tablecloth	goldfish bowl
arm	searchlights
hand	throne
footprint	siren
sun	tentacle
voice	field of snow
round head	ink stain
eyes	golden ball

Section B

Think of interesting comparisons for the nouns in Column A.

Write them in Column B.

Column A	Column B
cake	
cup	
feet	
table	
legs	
sandwich	
tea	
footprint	
stalks	

Choose six new nouns from the exemplar text. Write an interesting comparison for each one.

Practice in Writing Skills 2

Similes

A simile is a sentence that makes an imaginative comparison. It usually uses the word 'like' or 'as'.

Section A

Choose six interesting comparisons from Section A, Practice in Writing Skills 1. Make them into similes by writing them in sentences. The first one is done for you.

Josh's dirty footprint was like a black *ink stain*.

_____

_____

_____

_____

_____

_____

Section B

Complete these similes with ideas of your own.

The loud wind was like _____

The rain was like _____

Josh's mouth felt as dry as _____

The moon _____

His teeth _____

The sweet tea tasted like _____

The spacecraft was as big as _____

Make up five sentences in which you use similes about classroom objects.

Independent writing task

Write a chapter about Josh's discovery of a different imaginary world.
Use this guide to plan.

1. The part of Josh's house that leads to my imaginary world

2. What the world looked like
There may be something odd about what Josh first sees.

3. Who Josh found there
Perhaps use a made-up word for the characters.

4. The appearance of the inhabitants of my world
Make the characters strange. Supply interesting details.

5. What Josh saw in the place
Describe objects with something strange about them.

6. How I build up the atmosphere
Add expressive adjectives and phrases. Include a simile.

7. My extra piece of fantasy magic
Have some magical effects.

8. The final sentence
End in a strange way, so that the reader wonders what will happen.

9. The title of my chapter

Self-assessment

Read the story set in an imaginary world that you wrote. How well did you do? Tick the features you can see in it.

Name: _____	Date: _____

☐   My story is set in an imaginary place or time.
☐   I have make-believe characters.
☐   I have included magical effects.
☐   I have used expressive and descriptive language.
☐   I have used similes.
☐   My language creates atmosphere.

Next time, I would improve my story set in an imaginary world by …	Teacher's comment
	I have talked to my teacher about my work on stories set in an imaginary world. Pupil: _____ Teacher: _____

Changing Lives

Narrative: Stories from other cultures

Definition: *"Stories set in an unfamiliar place involving different ways of life."*

Lesson objective
To use settings and characterisation to engage readers' interest.

Warm up activity
- Enlarge, display and read aloud the exemplar text. Comment on the variety of punctuation.

- Explain that the extract is the beginning of a story. Ask: *What is the function of a story opening?* (To hook the reader.)

- Use talk partner and then class discussion to share ideas about if and how this story interests the reader. Identify points: curiosity about the unnamed place; interest in what will happen to the girl; concern about whether she will stay unhappy.

- Invite the class to vote: Does the opening succeed? Is the reader hooked?

Features

Unfamiliar settings

Character details

Different customs, beliefs, clothes or food

What to look out for

Expressive and descriptive language

Clear division into paragraphs

Varied punctuation

Writing investigation
Ask the children:
- Reread the text with a partner. Talk about its genre (a story from a different culture).

- Discuss with your partner which words helped you decide the genre. Circle two words. Choose three phrases or sentences to underline. They should all suggest the text's genre.

- Compare words with another pair of children and explain your choices. Have a class discussion and agree on three words for your teacher to circle and phrases or sentences to underline in the displayed text. (For example: circle *unfamiliar, different and figs*; underline *it was not a proper queue* and *this foreign land*.)

Independent writing
Ask the children:
- Identify the characters in the story. Share ideas with a partner for a list of four.

- Make a chart with three columns headed: character, what they are like, textual evidence. Draw six rows under the headings.

- Write these character names in the first four rows: Lara, Mother, passport official, the crowd. Discuss them with a partner and then fill in the chart. (Lara: nervous about moving; she did not want to live in this foreign land.)

- Write a paragraph with two new characters outside the airport building. Reveal information about them. Add their names and details to your chart.

Differentiation
- More confident writers may write two paragraphs with more detail.
- Less confident writers work with a partner and complete the chart about four characters only.

Plenary
Invite individual children to read out their paragraphs. Ask the class to identify new characters. What do they seem like? Which part of the text presents that picture? Ask the writer if that was what they intended. Work together on a new paragraph with interesting character details that confirm that the text is a story about another culture.

Changing Lives

The unfamiliar smell hit her as soon as she stepped from the plane. It was warm, stale and carried a mixture of foods: sweet oranges, over-ripe melons, rotting bananas, and sticky figs. The air made her cough; the glaring sun hurt her eyes. It all made Lara long for the cool freshness and gentle light of England.

Lethargically, already wearied by oppressive heat, she followed her mother across the tarmac into the airport building. In there, was a sea of noise. Everyone was shouting. People pushed and jostled one another. She struggled to find way through the crowds to keep up with her mother. At last they joined the passport queue. To Lara, it was not a proper queue. People did not stand one behind the other; they did not wait patiently. Instead, they struggled against one another, shouting their impatience and bickering over places.

Even Lara's mother seemed to have changed now they were here. When the passport official took her passport, she and the man spoke loudly and angrily to each other in the foreign language. At last, he nodded curtly, and threw down the book with disdain. When he turned to Lara, his manner changed. He smiled and pinched her cheek. Lara, close to tears of exhaustion, smiled weakly.

A minute later, she and her mother were waved past the control desk. After a final wait, their cases circled into view. Lara's mother snatched them eagerly, loaded their trolley and set off for the sign that Lara could not understand.

"Isn't it exciting?" said her mother. "They'll all be waiting for us outside. There'll be a big welcome home party for us tonight!"
"Home?" thought Lara bitterly. They were going to her mother's home, not hers! She did not want to live in this foreign land, miss her friends, and speak this new, shouting language. With a heavy heart, she realised how different this unwanted life was going to be.

Practice in Writing Skills 1

Semi-colons ➡ A semi-colon looks like this **;**
A semi-colon can link two sentences related to the same subject. A small letter is used after a semi-colon.

Section A

Make five sentences, using semi-colons to link pairs of sentences. The first one is done for you.

This was a hot part of the world. The temperature was always high. ➡

This was a hot part of the world; the temperature was always high.

Lara arrived in August. It was the hottest month.

_____

The weather made her tired. She could hardly walk.

_____

The language was difficult. Perhaps Lara would not learn it.

_____

The language was loud. People seemed to shout.

_____

Section B

Join up pairs of sentences to make five new sentences.

Use a semi-colon and make any necessary changes.

The girls travelled to school together on foot.

She did not want to tell them.

Lara had bad news for them.

The girls' routine was always the same.

There was the same food in their lunch boxes.

Lara was in a group of friends.

They never changed it.

They travelled back together by bus.

The friends were very happy.

Their drinks were the same too.

Practice in Writing Skills 2

Colons

A colon looks like this **:**
A colon is used to introduce more information.

Section A

Put the missing colon in each sentence. The first one is done for you.

Lara had three friends: Zoe, Sarah and Emma.

News went around the class Lara was leaving.

The teacher asked to speak to three girls Maisie, Sarah and Emma.

The girls went to town for one reason they had to buy a present.

They chose something special a photograph album.

Lara would take three special things pictures, words and memories.

- -

Section B

Use a colon to add a second half to each sentence. An example is done for you.

Ginny, the tame giraffe, had been there three years: the keepers hardly looked at her.

Her meal was always the same _____

The keeper came out with a dish _____

He called out _____

Ginny's response was rehearsed _____

Ginny's actions were practised _____

She acted strangely one day _____

Continue the story of Ginny with four sentences of your own using colons.

There is one colon in the extract 'Changing lives'. Copy the sentence containing it and explain its use.

Independent writing task

Write the opening pages of a story about a child in an unusual part of the world where people move often between places. Use this guide to help you plan.

1. The setting for my story Provide descriptive detail of an unfamiliar place. Gain the reader's interest by naming the country.	**2. My main character** Give the name, age and a description of what this child is wearing. Use interesting description.
3. Why they are moving Explain why the group is moving (perhaps extreme weather) and how the main character feels.	**4. What happens as they start off** Make something strange happen that would not happen where you live. It could be linked to the weather.
5. My last sentence Finish with the main character worried about the future. Your reader will want to read on.	**6. The title of my story**

Self-assessment

Read the story you wrote about another culture.
How well did you do? Tick the features you can see in it.

Name: _____ Date: _____

- ☐ My story has an unfamiliar setting.
- ☐ There are interesting details about my characters.
- ☐ I have mentioned different customs, clothes or food.
- ☐ I have used expressive and descriptive language.
- ☐ There is clear division into paragraphs.
- ☐ My punctuation is varied.
- ☐ My language creates atmosphere.

Next time, I would improve my story about another culture by ...	Teacher's comment

I have talked to my teacher about my work on stories from other cultures.

Pupil: _____

Teacher: _____

Charlotte's Web

Narrative: Stories which raise issues or dilemmas

Definition: *"Stories that look at difficult issues and how characters deal with them."*

Lesson objective

To consider an issue in a story and a character's dilemma.

Warm up activity

- Display and read aloud the enlarged text.
  Ask: *What issue is presented?* (Trapping flies.)

- Circle *sad, gloomily*. Why is Wilbur like this?
  (He disapproves of fly-trapping.)

- Define *dilemma*. (Having to make a decision when both choices have disadvantages.)
  Ask: *What is Charlotte's dilemma?* (Should I trap insects?)
  What does she decide? (Yes.)

Features

A problem or issue

First and second person pronouns

Resolution of the dilemma

What to look out for

Character involvement

Emotion

A dilemma

Writing investigation
Ask the children:

- Identify words or phrases that show Charlotte's belief that she is right to trap flies. Compare choices with your partner. (*Not a bad pitch, live by my wits, sharp, clever, shaking one of her legs*.)

- Read Charlotte's main speech. Circle references to herself. (*I, me, my*) In a different colour, circle references to Wilbur. (*you, my friend*) Underline *shaking one of her legs*. What does this emphasise? (Strong feeling and emphatic speech.)

- Take turns with your partner being Charlotte and reading this long speech aloud. Discuss the effect the circled words have on the listener, Wilbur.

- Share results with the class. Agree that Charlotte makes the issue personal with the words *I, me* and *my*. By using *you* and *my friend*, she involves Wilbur, making him think how he would resolve the dilemma.

Independent writing
Ask the children:

- Read the two sentences '*You …feeds me*'. Discuss with a partner Charlotte's criticism of Wilbur. Write the issue in your own words. (Wilbur does not find his food.)

- Pretend to be Wilbur. Write your dilemma in the form of a question. (For example: *Should I accept the food brought to me?*)

- Write two headings *Yes* and *No*. Under each, write a bad consequence of that decision. (If you take the food, other animals may think you lazy. If you refuse, you may go hungry.) Tick your decision.

- Write a paragraph of speech in which you, as Wilbur, tell Charlotte your decision. Be persuasive by using *I* and *you*.

Differentiation

- More confident writers may write at greater length and add Charlotte's reply.
- Less confident writers work with a partner and use the paragraph opener supplied.

Plenary

Write Wilbur's dilemma question on the whiteboard and discuss its consequences. Ask the children to vote. Invite children, as Wilbur, to read their speech. Are listening children, as Charlotte, persuaded and involved?

Charlotte's Web

'All our family have been trappers.
Way back for thousands and thousands of years we spiders have been laying for flies and bugs.'
'It's a miserable inheritance,' said Wilbur, gloomily.
He was sad because his new friend was so bloodthirsty.
'Yes, it is,' agreed Charlotte. 'But I can't help it. I don't know how the first spider in the early days of the world happened to think up this fancy idea of spinning a web, but she did, and it was clever of her, too. And since then, all of us spiders have had to work the same trick. It's not a bad pitch, on the whole.'
'It's cruel,' replied Wilbur, who did not intend to be argued out of this position.
'Well, you can't talk,' said Charlotte.
'You have your meals brought to you in a pail. Nobody feeds me. I have to get my own living. I live my wits. I have to be sharp and clever, lest I go hungry. I have to think things out, catch what I can, take what comes. And it just so happens, my friend, that what comes is flies and insects and bugs. And furthermore,' said Charlotte, shaking one of her legs, ' do you realize that if I didn't catch bugs and eat them, bugs would increase and multiply and get so numerous that they'd destroy the earth, wipe out everything?'
'Really?' said Wilbur. "I wouldn't want that to happen.
Perhaps your web is a good thing after all.'

Practice in Writing Skills 1

Direct speech

> Direct speech means putting the words spoken inside inverted commas (often called quotation marks or speech marks).
> ✓ The first spoken word in a sentence always begins with a capital letter.
> ✓ Spoken words and unspoken words must be kept apart by a comma, question mark or exclamation mark.
> ✓ Each speaker has a new paragraph.

Section A

Put all the missing punctuation in each sentence. The first one is done for you.

"I'm pleased to meet you," said Charlotte.

i hope we can be friends continued charlotte

how long have you lived here asked wilbur

quite a long time replied charlotte

wilbur asked do you have many friends

oh everyone is friendly here exclaimed Charlotte

Section B

Make up a sentence for each animal character to say. Use the phrase in the bubble. Remember, you need a punctuation mark separating the spoken words from the rest of the sentence.

called Charlotte.

Templeton piped up

Wilbur exclaimed

Lucy suggested

repeated the goose.

grumbled the horse.

_____

_____

_____

_____

_____

_____

Write six sentences, each containing speech, for a conversation between a rat and a sheep.

Practice in Writing Skills 2

First person writing → Writing in the first person means that the writers or speakers use pronouns that refer to themselves.
(Pronouns are words that stand in place of nouns.)
Personal pronouns: _I_, _me_, _we_, _us_
Possessive pronouns: _mine, ours_

Section A

Retell this story in the first person as if you are Wilbur, talking. The first sentence is done for you.

~~Wilbur feels sad~~. He does not like what is happening. The fault is not his! He did not know that the spider was bloodthirsty! However, the problem is now his. He needs to think. What will the answer be for him? He will tell you later.

I feel sad. _____

_____

_____

_____

_____

_____

_____

_____

_____

_____

_____

_____

_____

Section B

Retell this story in the first person as if you are Wilbur, talking. You will need to use plural as well as singular pronouns. The first sentence is done for you.

~~Wilbur has decided.~~ They will be friends! They will do lots of things together. There will be different meal arrangements for them. Wilbur will not trap flies! They will still have different ways of getting food. Charlotte can trap food while Wilbur watches. That is not the way for Wilbur! His will be brought to him in a bucket.

"I have decided _____

_____

_____

_____

_____

_____

_____

_____

_____

_____

_____

_____

Independent writing task

Stories or dilemmas → Write a new chapter of the story. Make it about Wilbur and Templeton, the rat. Think of an issue, plan a dilemma and reveal what Wilbur decided and said to Templeton.

1. The start of my chapter Perhaps Templeton, the cunning rat, has said that wants to be Wilbur's friend.	**2. What the issue was** Maybe Templeton was clever but greedy.
3. What Wilbur's dilemma was He may have to decide whether to let Templeton share his meals.	**4. What Wilbur decided** Explain the consequences of his decision.
5. What Wilbur said to Templeton to explain his decision Put strong feelings into quite a long speech. Make sure that Wilbur speaks in the first person and uses words that make Templeton feel involved.	**6. What Templeton said in reply** Let Templeton agree with Wilbur.

7. The title of my chapter

Self-assessment

Stories or dilemmas

Read the story you wrote about an issue or dilemma.
How well did you do? Tick the features you can see in it.

Name: _____   Date: _____

- ☐ My story has a problem or issue.
- ☐ Characters face a dilemma.
- ☐ The dilemma is sorted out.
- ☐ I have expressed the feelings of characters.
- ☐ I have used some first person writing, as the writer or the speaker.
- ☐ I have made the reader or the character spoken to feel involved.
- ☐ I have used first and second person pronouns.

Next time, I would improve my story about an issue or dilemma by...

Teacher's comment

I have talked to my teacher about my work on stories which raise issues or dilemmas.

Pupil: _____

Teacher: _____

Facing Changes

Narrative: Plays

Definition: *"Telling stories through the words that characters say."*

Lesson objective
To explore characteristics of play scripts.

Warm up activity

- Display the text 'Changing Lives' on page 21 for the children to scan. Point out how the text's story is told mainly through narrative.

- Question the children about how this story could be told in the form of a play.
  Ask: *Who are the main characters?* (Lara and her mother.)

- Reread paragraph one. Put the children into pairs as Lara and her mother, to act and improvise speech for this paragraph.

- Ask: *What form of narrative have you used?* (A play).
  How did you invent your speech? (Using description in the story.)

Features

Stage directions in brackets and, usually, in italics

Layout that is easy to use

Colon after character's name

What to look out for

No speech marks

Character's name in bold capital letters

New line for different speeches

Distinction between character's name and his/her words

Writing investigation
Ask the children:

- Look at the exemplar text. Identify the text type. (Play.)

- Join three other children. With two children acting as all the passengers, take parts and read the script aloud. Identify:
  · Four stage directions. How did you know not to say them? (Italics and brackets.)
  · Punctuation telling you how to speak. (Exclamation marks.)
  · Three differences between this speech writing and story dialogue. (No speech marks; no 'said' verbs; clear distinction between a character's name and his/her words.)

- Compare the two narrative forms: the story 'Changing Lives' on page 21 and this playscript. At which point in the story does the playscript stop? (The end of paragraph two.) Share answers as a class.

Independent writing
Ask the children:

- Reread the rest of the story 'Changing Lives' (*Even Lara's* to the end).

- In groups of three, discuss a playscript for this part of the story and how to divide it into two scenes.

- Improvise dialogue as you act the scenes.

- Write some of your playscript, with stage directions.

Differentiation
- More confident writers write a complete scene.
- Less confident writers write only a few speeches.

Plenary

Let pairs perform a scene for another pair. Encourage constructive feedback. Model on the whiteboard changing some of the story to a playscript. Enlist help with stage directions.

Facing Changes

Cast of characters:

Lara (nine-year-old girl)

Mrs Pietroni (Lara's mother)

Passport official

Passengers (a crowd)

Grandma Simoni (Mrs Pietroni's mother)

Grandpa Anthos (Mrs Pietroni's father)

Scene 1: Outside the plane

MRS PIETRONI: (*Helping Lara down last steps from plane*) Come on, Lara! Watch where you're going!

LARA: (*shielding her eyes*) I can't see properly.

MRS PIETRONI: You'll soon get used to this bright sun. It makes a lovely change after our dreary London days.

LARA: (*Sulkily*) It's too hot here. I like the weather in London.

MRS PIETRONI: It's perfect for me.

LARA: And another thing! This air's making me cough. (*Clearing throat noisily*)

MRS PIETRONI: Don't be silly! You're doing that on purpose!

LARA: (*Wrinkling her nose and pulling a face*) Ugh! What's that revolting smell?

MRS PIETRONI: What smell?

LARA: A nasty smell! Like when we keep our fruit too long. You know, sickly sweet oranges, squashy melons, rotting bananas and your horrible, sticky figs!

MRS PIETRONI: It all smells wonderful. Now stop grumbling and follow me.

(*Mrs Pietroni leads them across the tarmac towards the airport building.*)

Scene 2: Inside the airport terminal

(*Passengers call out, talking over one another.*)

PASSENGER 1: Let me through!

PASSENGER 2: Hurry up!

PASSENGER 3: This way! This way!

PASSENGER 4: Use your elbows!

PASSENGER 5: Out of my way!

LARA: (*Calling to her mother ahead*) Mum, I can't keep up with you! It's too crowded! I can't get through!

MRS PIETRONI: (*Looking back and shouting*) Come on, Lara! Just push your way through.

A moment later …

LARA: Why are we standing here?

MRS PIETRONI: It's the passport queue, of course.

LARA: (*Amazed*) This isn't a proper queue! People in England stand one behind the other!

(*Passengers are shouting impatiently and pushing against one another.*)

PASSENGER 1: That's my place!

PASSENGER 2: I'm next!

PASSENGER 3: (*Waving passport*) Check this! Check this!

PASSENGER 4: Out of the way! Out of the way!

PASSENGER 5: Squeeze in there!

MRS PIETRONI: (*Shouting impatiently*) We're next! We're next!

LARA: (*Confused*) Why does everyone push and shout here? And people keep taking my place!

MRS PIETRONI: (*Smiling happily*) It's different here, Lara. You'll get used to it.

Adverbs

Adverbs add interest and detail. They often end in -ly.
When used within a sentence, they are often placed just after the verb.
Adverbs may answer these questions:
How? When? Where? How often?

Section A

Work with a partner to decide which question each adverb answers. Then write the adverb in the correct box. The first one is done for you.

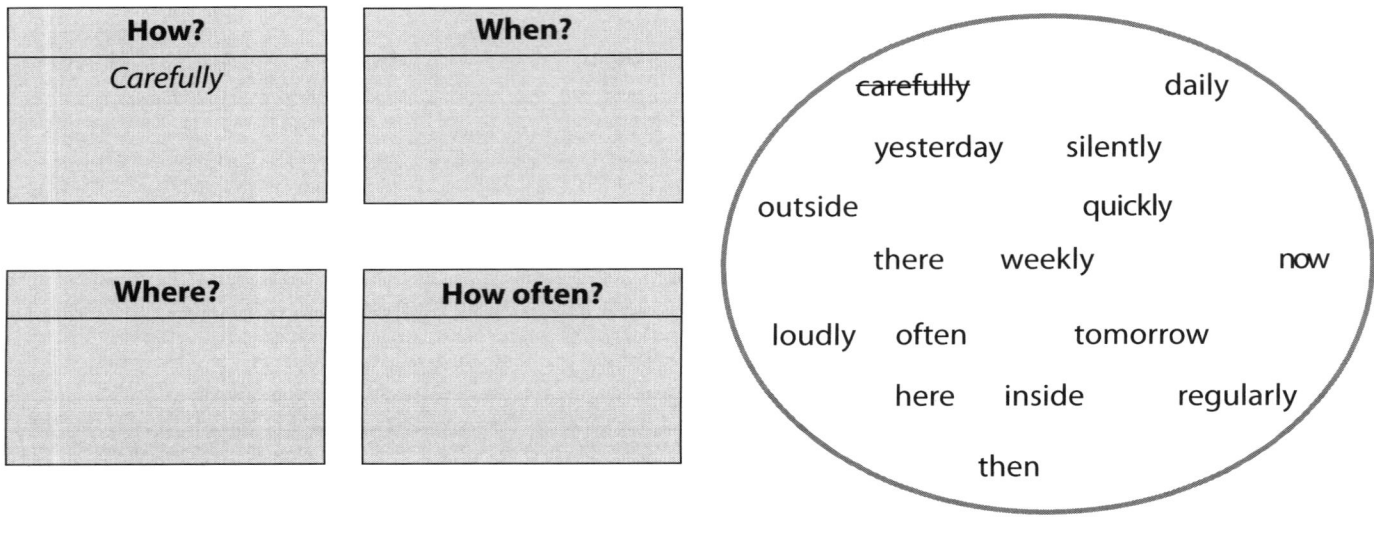

How?	When?
Carefully	

Where?	How often?

Words in the circle: carefully, daily, yesterday, silently, outside, quickly, there, weekly, now, loudly, often, tomorrow, here, inside, regularly, then

Section B

Use the Where? and How often? adverbs from Section A. Use and underline each in a sentence.

Afterwards write the verb it adds information to. An example is done for you.

A grateful Lara drinks *greedily*! (drinks)

_____

_____

_____

_____

_____

_____

_____

_____

Practice in Writing Skills 2

Apostrophes to mark contraction

➤ An apostrophe may help to make writing sound more natural by shortening words into contractions.
In contractions, an apostrophe replaces those letters that are left out. This apostrophe of omission is used in informal writing and written speech.

Section A

These apostrophes show that letters have been left out. Write the missing letters in the kites.

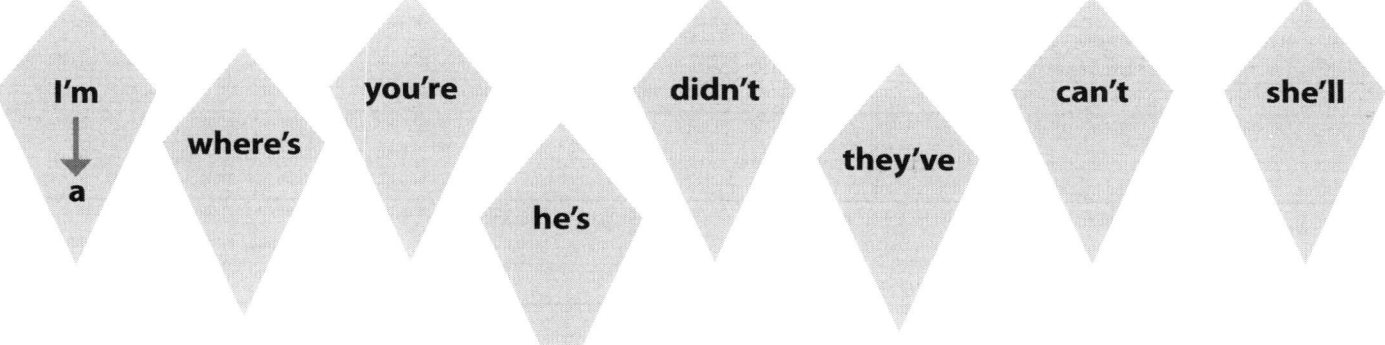

I'm → a
where's
you're
he's
didn't
they've
can't
she'll

Section B

Read the two jigsaw words aloud, pushing them together as you speak. Write the contraction in the empty jigsaw piece. The first one is done for you.

she is — she's
you will
I have
it is
who is
we have
did not
she had
he will
they will

Independent writing task

Narrative Plays

Write two new scenes for 'Facing Changes'. Set them outside the airport building. Involve Lara, Mrs Pietroni, Grandma Simoni and Grandpa Anthos.

1. What will happen in Scene 5 Write short notes. Give Lara some problems with her grandparents.	**2. Setting for the scene**
3. After rehearsing some words, this is my dialogue for Scene 5 Remember not to use speech marks. Write on a different page.	**4. What will happen in Scene 6** Write short notes. Make Lara happier about her changed life.
5. Setting for the scene This could be Lara's school.	**6. After rehearsing some words, this is my dialogue for Scene 6** Check the layout. Write on another page.
7. Useful contractions Reading aloud will help you spot where your words do not sound natural. Use apostrophes.	**8. Places for my stage directions** Put the directions within brackets; keep them short; do not have too many.

Self-assessment

Read the play script you wrote. How well did you do? Tick the features you can see in it.

Name: _____ Date: _____

☐   The layout is easy to follow.
☐   I distinguish between a character's name and his/her words.
☐   The character's name is on the left.
☐   I have a colon after the character's name.
☐   The character's name is in bold capitals.
☐   I start a new line for different speeches.
☐   I have not used speech marks.
☐   My stage directions are within brackets.

Next time, I would improve my playscript by ...	Teacher's comment
	I have talked to my teacher about my work on plays. Pupil: _____ Teacher: _____

The Game and the Leader

Narrative: Fantasy adventures

Definition: *"A story that brings fantasy to life."*

Lesson objective
To show imagination through the language used to create emphasis, humour, atmosphere or suspense.

Warm up activity
- Display and read aloud the exemplar text.

- Ask: *What type of narrative does this extract seem to be?* Let partners exchange answers before you accept answers from the class. Conclude that an impossible happening makes the text fantasy; investigating the unknown makes it also an adventure.

- Ask the children if they have read other stories with this pattern. Share ideas, commenting on the mixture of reality and fantasy, for example, in 'Tom's Midnight Garden'; 'Harry Potter'; 'Pippi Longstocking'; 'The Lion, the Witch and the Wardrobe'.

Features

Real and imaginary characters

Interesting situation

Excitement or fear

A tense atmosphere

What to look out for

Growing suspense

Incredible happenings

Elements of magic

Expressive and descriptive language

Cliffhanger moments

Writing investigation
Ask the children:

- Discuss the four characters in the text with your partner. Divide the characters into two types. What two labels could you apply? (Human and imaginary.) Which characters belong to which column?

- Read aloud the paragraph from *Immediately*… to… *figure* while your partner draws what they 'see'. Exchange roles and afterwards compare pictures.

- Investigate the language responsible for details of your pictures, identifying three powerful verbs. (*burst, radiated, tumbled, raining, clustered.*) Which simile created a vivid image for you? (… *stars tumbled from the top of the screen as if raining from an unseen cloud.*)

Independent writing
Ask the children:

- Read the text. Find the verbs *groaned* and *sneered*. Whose speech do they describe? What do they tell the reader about this boy's attitude to Professor Smith's computer games?

- Which boy is ashamed of the start of Professor's program? Which adjective tells you this? (*embarrassed.*) Which revealing verb is used about his speech? (*mumbled*).

- Reread the final paragraph. How does it make you feel? (Wondering about what will happen.) What is this type of ending called? (Cliffhanger.)

Differentiation
- More confident writers may investigate the image created of Professor Smith and which words are important.
- Less confident writers work with a partner and may need to be reminded of the word 'cliffhanger'.

Plenary
Share and discuss the children's answers. Put the children into pairs to talk about another cliffhanger ending to a story or chapter they have read. Invite them to tell the class about it.

The Game and the Leader

"Do me a favour, Dex!" called out Professor Smith as he was leaving for his evening class. "Try out my new game for me. I need to send the disk off tomorrow. It's on my desk."

Professor Smith taught science at the local college. He was also a genius with computers. In his spare time, he wrote computer games for Fantasmania. He always gave the games a final run through before he sent them to the company. However, with the deadline for the next game so near, he would have to rely on nine-year-old Dexter to do the check this time.

Dexter rang up his friend Solomon and invited him over. Within ten minutes, both boys were sitting in front of a large interactive whiteboard. With the disk loaded in the computer, they were ready to start.
"Right," said Dexter as he clicked an icon, "let's see what Dad's done this time."

Immediately, the screen burst into life. A spinning ball of light radiated from the centre and covered the screen. Tiny stars tumbled from the top of the screen as if raining from an unseen cloud. Gradually, the stars clustered together to create the form of a figure.
"Of course," groaned Solomon. "Prof Smith's favourite! A wizard!"
"I've told Dad to think of something different," mumbled Dexter, embarrassed. "The company will stop buying his games if they all start in the same way."
"Good evening," greeted a voice. "Welcome to you both. May I take you to meet my leader?"
"Yes! Yes!" chorused the boys.

The wizard waved his wand and stretched out a gloved hand. Half of the hand seemed to come out from the screen.
"That's obviously a 3-D trick," sneered Solomon.
"Touch his hand, Sol," pleaded Dexter.

Solomon touched the hand. He felt himself being pulled! Dexter watched in disbelieving excitement and horror as his friend's body moved into the screen.

Practice in Writing Skills 1

Adjectives made from suffixes →

Adjectives can be formed by the addition of a suffix (a group of letters) to a base word.

fear (base word) + *less* (suffix) = *fearless* (adjective)

Section A

Copy out these word sums and write their adjective answers. The first one is done for you.

wonder + ful = *wonderful*

occasion + al =

fear + less =

speed + y =

trick + y =

sensation + al =

Use each of the new adjectives you have made in a sentence.

_____

_____

_____

_____

_____

_____

_____

_____

Section B

Look at the adjectives highlighted. Write them as a word sums and answers. The first one is done for you.

Be careful! That material may be <u>breakable</u>.

break + able = *breakable*

The wizard has a red face and tearful eyes.

_____

What a messy place!

_____

I think that he is a hopeless juggler

_____

Please stop showing off and being boastful.

_____

The wizard is noisy.

_____

The Leader is speechless!

_____

We need to be careful.

_____

Practice in Writing Skills 2

Verb tenses

Verbs may be in a past, present or future tense.
I _looked_ (past)
I _look_ (present)
I _will look_ (future)

Section A

Identify the tense of the verb underlined and write if it is past, present or future.

In the last two sentences, you must also do the underlining.

Professor Smith <u>starts</u> today.   _present_

He <u>will be</u> very busy.

The professor <u>made</u> so many lists yesterday.

Today he <u>feels</u> organised.

He looks nervous, though.

The game will last two hours.

Make a chart of three columns: past, present and future. Choose 10 verbs from the exemplar text to write in the 'past' column. Fill in their present and future forms.

Section B

These past and present verbs are jumbled. Write them in jigsaw pairs. Put a red dot on the present tense jigsaw pieces and a blue dot on the past tense jigsaw pieces.

I spoke	I grew	I talked
I know	I see	I helped
I help	I knew	I saw
I talk	I looked	I look
I grow	I speak	

Independent writing task

Write the next chapter of the fantasy adventure 'The Game and the Leader'. Use this guide to help you plan.

1. My characters
Keep the boys and the wizard. Introduce one or two new characters.

2. My interesting situation
Where are both boys? What are they trying to do?

3. The mood of excitement or fear
Who is excited or afraid? What do they do or say to reveal this? Use dialogue and powerful verbs.

4. My incredible happenings
Make some events difficult to believe.

5. Magical effects
Do not have too much magic.

6. Expressive descriptions
Bring a scene to life with well-chosen adjectives and verbs. A simile may be effective.

7. My cliffhanger ending
Finish with exciting uncertainty so that the reader wants to read the next chapter.

Self-assessment

Fantasy adventures

Read the fantasy adventure story that you wrote. How well did you do? Tick the features you can see in it.

Name: _____	Date: _____

☐   My story has real and imaginary characters.
☐   I have used an interesting situation.
☐   There is excitement or fear.
☐   The atmosphere is sometimes tense.
☐   My story's suspense grows.
☐   My plot has incredible happenings.
☐   I have included magical effects.
☐   I have used expressive and descriptive language.
☐   I have created a cliffhanger moment.

Next time, I would improve my fantasy adventure by ...	Teacher's comment
	I have talked to my teacher about my work on fantasy adventures.
	Pupil: _____
	Teacher: _____

ENGLAND CONQUERS!

Non-fiction: Recounts – newspapers/magazines

Definition: *"Retelling an event or series of events."*

Lesson objective
To shape material and ideas to write a convincing and informative non-narrative text.

Warm up activity
- Let partners tell each other what 'fact' and 'opinion' mean. Agree on definitions to write on the whiteboard.

- Display and read aloud the exemplar text. Where would they find this text? (Newspaper.)

- Circle *Yesterday*, *reached*, *remained*, *battled*. Ask: *What do these words tell you?* (The text is about the past.)

- Identify this as a recount text. Can the children explain why? (Past events are retold.)

Features

Appropriate writing style and tone for the reader

An introduction

Chronological order

Essential words

What to look out for

Past tense

1st or 3rd person writing

A closing statement

Language to suit the subject

Connectives (particularly time connectives)

Writing investigation
Ask the children:

- Reread the exemplar text with a partner. Is it mainly fact or opinion? (Fact.)

- Put two headings: 'fact' and 'opinion'. Write two examples of each from the text. (Facts: names, score, occasion, actions, individuals' quoted words. Opinions: views on managers, their ability, players' attitude and skill, fans' feelings.

- Time connectives form important links in recount texts. Identify two examples. (*Early on; meanwhile.*)

- Discuss with your partner how the journalist wrote her text. Which parts needed accuracy? (Names, scores and quotes.) Did she probably make notes first? Share ideas as a class. Work with your teacher on a list of notes that Sarah wrote while watching the first half. (Hot, sticky. Rue du Parc. 1st half: quiet play – supporters keen, cheering; then angry – misses booed; – players shouted at – jeering at referee.)

Independent writing
Ask the children:

- Remember that notes are informal in language, layout and punctuation, but must make sense to the writer afterwards.

- Imagine that Sarah Khan has some unused notes. (Additional details of the game, somebody sent off, or another interview.) Discuss ideas with a partner before you write Sarah's extra notes.

- The newspaper editor has extra space! Write up your notes as text. Decide where to place the text and use a time connective to make a smooth link.

Differentiation
- More confident writers write at greater length.
- Less confident writers do writing work with a partner.

Plenary
Ask children to read their text aloud. Can listeners identify it as fact or opinion? Is its style appropriate?

ENGLAND CONQUERS!

By Sarah Khan, Assistant Sports Writer

Yesterday afternoon, in sticky August heat, the Football World Cup Tournament reached its climax. Only two teams remained: England and Spain. At Paris's Rue du Parc, they battled for the World Cup.

Early on, both teams seemed overawed by the occasion and supporters' expectations. At first, fans roared approval of every near-miss, but towards half-time they looked and sounded impatient. Missed goals were booed, players were taunted and the referee was jeered at.

"Everyone's just bored!" remarked the BBC television commentator, Jamie Allsop, at half-time. "England must work harder!"

Maybe England's manager, Harry Ranger, heard him. After half-time, he substituted Robson for Stiles; he swapped over the wingers; and he pushed Tooney forward to support Gary Norvick. The team was energised! Five minutes later, Tooney scored a superb goal.

Meanwhile, Spain was also changing. Pedros replaced an unfit-looking Thasos; Wenri moved back into defence; and Ronaldi switched to the left wing. When England scored, Spain's manager, Fabio Pacellos, could be seen shouting more instructions and gesturing from the touchline.

"I don't think jumping up and down will help them!" scoffed Jamie Allsop.

Maybe he was wrong. Whatever Pacellos said worked. Immediately, Spain changed tactics:

Ronaldi roamed freely and the attacking moves seemed faster. After ten minutes, Ronaldi headed a ball into the net.

For the final 20 minutes, the teams stayed level. As they battled, energy flagged, legs succumbed to cramp, and extra play and penalties loomed. Then England broke the stalemate. Rio Giggs dribbled down the wing. Tooney, stayed level. When Giggs passed, all Tooney had to do was slot the ball home. England was ahead again.

After that, England looked determined not to surrender their lead. With the fans roaring encouragement, the team defended every pass. Spain could find no way through. When the final whistle blew, the score stood at 2-1.

Interviewed on the pitch afterwards, an emotional Ryan Robson, England's captain, said, "I can't believe it! England has won the World Cup."

Practice in Writing Skills 1

Time connectives

Connectives link words or sentences. They help hold text together. Time connectives emphasise chronology (time sequence) in the text.
First the children did their homework.
Immediately afterwards, they set off for the park.

Section A

Underline the time connective in each sentence. The first one is done for you.

<u>Within minutes,</u> Sarah had joined a traffic queue.

After an hour, she was still there.

That afternoon, she had her first big job.

For a while, she watched the clock.

Then the traffic started to move.

At last, she was on her way!

Immediately, she felt happier.

Soon she would be there.

Section B

Underline the connective in each sentence.

Meanwhile the clock was ticking.

Just in time Sarah arrived at the football stadium.

At first she was confused by the French signs.

Then she recognised another sports journalist.

After that she was fine.

Soon she was sitting in the journalist' box.

Straightaway she got out her pencil and notebook.

Two minutes later the match began.

At the same time she started her career as a reporter.

Now read the sentences aloud. If you hear a pause, place a comma there.

Use these time connectives in sentences of your own about Sarah Khan.

Check whether commas are needed.

beforehand; later on; within the hour; some time later; finally; prior to that; afterwards

Practice in Writing Skills 2

A *hyphen* looks like this -
It emphasises the connection between two words.

A *dash* is longer –
It is used in informal writing to introduce another thought on the same topic.
The hard-hearted referee annoyed the crowd – he blew his whistle for anything.

Section A

Underline the conjunction in each sentence.

The first one is done for you.

Sarah was not well-off.

However, she was well qualified.

The Editor was rather ill tempered.

He gave Sarah a second hand car to use.

She had to set out for the match at lunch time.

Suppose there was a hold up!

Divide these sentences with a dash. The first one is done for you.

Sarah had to drive carefully – the car was old.

Then she lost her way the car had no map.

She stopped at a garage the owners were bound to know the way,

She asked for directions she was desperate.

Unfortunately, the owners were French they spoke only French.

Section B

Take pairs of words from the box and join them with a hyphen.

spoken	silver	plated
empty	rope	scratched
badly	faced	headed
room	sitting	two
skipping	clearly	

Add 5 dashes to the paragraph below.

Sarah realised that the garage owners could not understand her. The she had an idea it was a brainwave! She took her notepad and pencil from her bag. She drew a footballer she put an England flag with him. Opposite him, she drew a footballer with a French flag. At the bottom of the page she drew her car it was clearly hers. She drew herself with a confused expression. She also put a question mark in the space between her car and the players this was important. The owners understood! They grabbed her pad it was proving so useful. They drew a perfect map for her.

Independent writing task

Recounts

You are a sports reporter for the local newspaper and have been sent to report on an important school match.
Write notes as you watch the game.
Later, use your notes and this guide to write a newspaper recount.
Use a computer for your final version.

1. My headline Make it attention-grabbing in large font.	**2. My subheading** Put it just below the headline in slightly smaller font.
3. Byline Put your name and your job.	**4. My introduction** In a short paragraph write what, where and when the match was, and who played. Remember to use the past tense.
5. Paragraphs with some details of the match in the order they happened Think about what readers will want to know: how individuals performed, important incidents, special times in the match.	**6. Include vivid language** Use descriptions to suit the sport.
7. Have one or two quotes Choose important people so readers are interested.	**8. My closing statement** Mention future possibilities or use a final quote for an effective ending.

Self-assessment

Recounts → Read the newspaper recount you wrote. How well did you do? Tick the features you can see in it.

Name: _____ Date: _____

- ☐ My recount has an introduction.
- ☐ I have used essential words.
- ☐ The events are in chronological order.
- ☐ I have written in the 1st or 3rd person.
- ☐ My recount is in the past tense.
- ☐ I have included time connectives.
- ☐ My writing style and tone are appropriate for the reader.
- ☐ I have used language that suits my subject.
- ☐ I have a closing statement.

Next time, I would improve my newspaper recount by ...	Teacher's comment
	I have talked to my teacher about my work on recounts. Pupil: _____ Teacher: _____

Roman houses

Non-fiction: Information texts

Definition: *"A text that presents facts clearly, using a variety of formats."*

Lesson objective
To summarise and shape material and ideas from different sources to write convincing and informative non-narrative texts.

Warm up activity
- Display and read aloud the exemplar text.

- Discuss the text's purpose. Agree that it informs the reader about the houses of wealthy Romans. Identify it as an information text.

- Invite the children to consider how the writer first set about writing it. Encourage partner before class discussion. Agree on the need for the writer to have information.

- Ask partners to list two types of information sources that the writer could have used. Let the children hold up their answers for a class comparison. Write a list of information sources on the board. (History texts; pictures and their captions; diagrams and their labels; Internet websites.)

Features

Labels

Introduction

Appropriate format

Captions ← **What to look out for**

Key words

Subheadings

Clear layout

Illustrations and diagrams

Writing investigation
Ask the children:
- Examine the text and point out the words in bold font for your teacher to circle. Discuss with your partner why they are in bold font. Can you think of three reasons? (Title; subheadings; key words; entries for the book's glossary.)

- Investigate the labels and captions with the picture and diagram. Discuss with your partner why they are needed. Do they add information?

- Reread the text. What tense is it written in? (Past.) Do you think that an information text is always in this tense? Share your thoughts with a partner. (The present tense is more usual. The past tense is used here for historical information.)

Independent writing
Ask the children:
- Pick out the six words for the book's glossary. List them in alphabetical order and write a brief definition for each.

- Reread the section entitled 'Inside'. Suppose that the writer wants to divide this text (from *You first entered …* to *peristyle*) differently, using three paragraphs and three subheadings. Decide on the divisions.

- Rewrite this part of the text with the subheadings.

Differentiation
- More confident writers do research and add text and a diagram with additional information about Roman houses.
- Less confident writers do writing work with a partner.

Plenary

Compare the children's new paragraph divisions and subheadings in their revised texts. Revise alphabetical order. How did the children decide whether to start their glossary with *atrium* or *aqueduct*? (Alphabetical order of the second letters.)

Roman houses

Wealthy Romans lived in spacious houses that were designed to give privacy and protection. These villas also provided beauty, space and comfort.

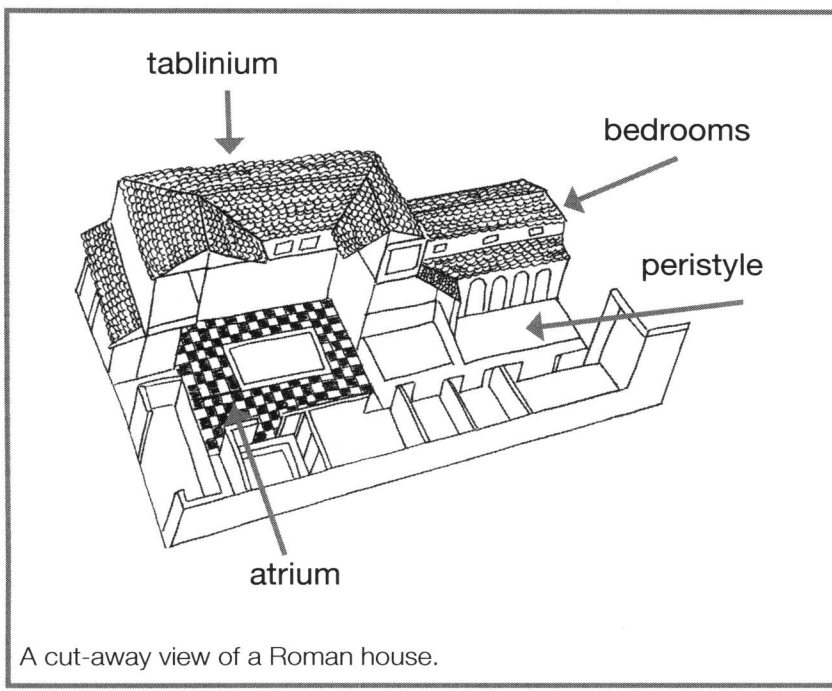

A cut-away view of a Roman house.

Outside

Houses faced inwards and they had few outside windows. So, from the outside, the houses looked very bare. This was for the owner's privacy and safety from burglary.

Inside

You first entered an indoor courtyard called an **atrium**. This was the house's entrance hall. The atrium was open to the sky, so it let in light. Beneath this opening was a basin to collect rainwater. This basin was the household's water supply. In later years, the basin was unnecessary because **aqueducts** were built and brought running water to the house.

Rooms were placed around the atrium. A particularly important room was the **tablinium**. It was the head of the family's 'office' and the room where he would welcome visitors. Behind the tablinium there was usually a garden with flowers and statues. Some houses had a garden with a covered walkway round its edges. The walkway's shade protected people from the hot sun. This type of garden was called a **peristyle**.

Walls and floors

The house's inside walls were often brightly-decorated. They were painted with pictures of gods, heroes, **gladiators**, animals, fish, countryside, and scenes of hunting and farming. The floors' decorations were beautiful **mosaics**, pictures made up of tiny tiles that had been pressed into the floor when the cement was still wet.

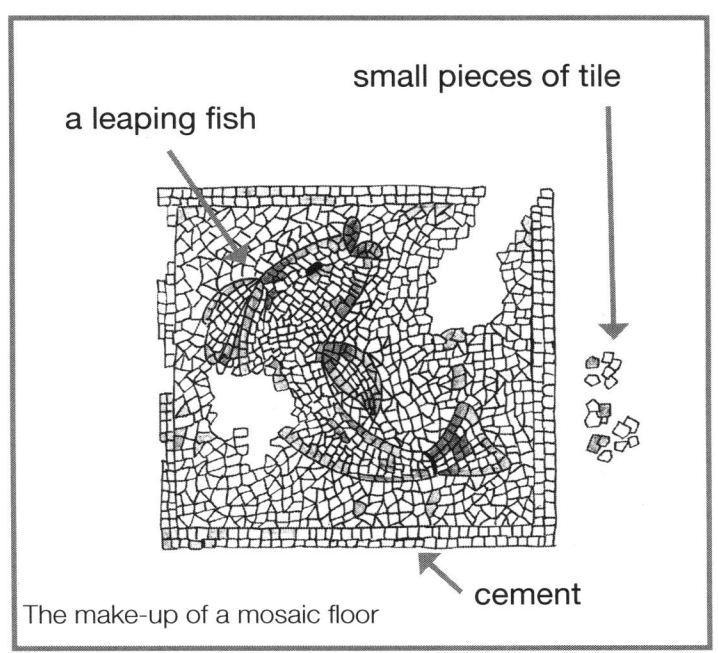

The make-up of a mosaic floor

Practice in Writing Skills 1

Alphabetical order → *Alphabetical order* means following the sequence of the alphabet. The first letter of words, and sometimes later letters, must be considered.

Section A

Write these lines of words in alphabetical order. If words begin with the same letter, look at their second letter as well. The first line is done for you.

house, beautiful, space, owner, comfortable ➜
beautiful, comfortable, house, owner, space

spices, kitchen, cook, meal, room
water, quiet, safety, peaceful, light,
slave, banquet, jug, meat, wine,
wealthy, rural, food, rich, feast,
picture, fish, animals, floor, tile
people, horses, walls, heroes, painted
decoration, bright, indoor, basin, hall

Section B

Put the 's' and 't' sections of the book's index into alphabetical order. You will need to look at first second, third and fourth letters.

stable	
Senator	
tile	
security	
shade	
tablet	
sunlight	
toga	
Senate	
town	
sage	
thyme	
storehouse	
tablinium	

Make up the 'v' and 'w' sections in the index of a book about Romans.

Practice in Writing Skills 2

An apostrophe can indicate ownership.
The <u>cat's</u> collar was missing.
An apostrophe may be a short way to explain ownership.
For example, it is quicker to write *'the cat's collar'* than *'the collar belonging to the cat'*.
The apostrophe's position varies according to the owner.
singular: *the <u>cat's</u> bowl* (the owner is one cat)
plural: *the <u>cats'</u> bowl* (the owners are two or more cats)

*Remember: the apostrophe is always placed after the owner's name.

Section A

Match these phrases about singular owners.

Pair a long phrase with a shorter one using an apostrophe. The first one is done for you.

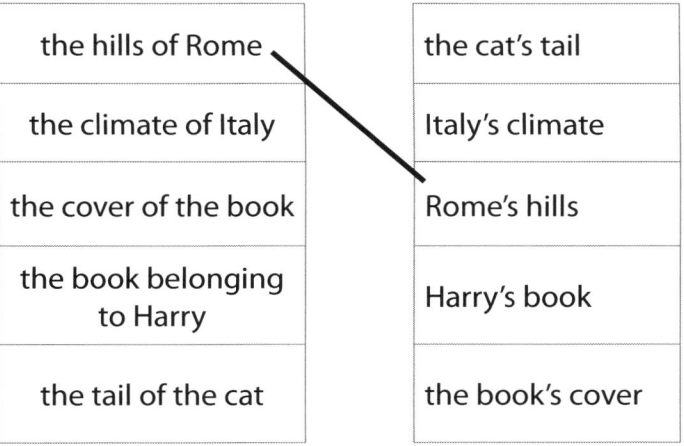

the hills of Rome	the cat's tail
the climate of Italy	Italy's climate
the cover of the book	Rome's hills
the book belonging to Harry	Harry's book
the tail of the cat	the book's cover

Match these phrases about plural owners.

Pair a long phrase with a shorter one using an apostrophe.

the windows of the houses	the children's books
the heat of those places	the houses' windows
the covers of the books	the books' covers
the books belonging to the children	the cats' tails
the tails of the cats	those places' heat

Section B

There are two plural owners in each line.

Circle them.

the witches' spells; the boy's pet; the children's clothes; the wizard's wand;

the author's stories; the dogs' eyes; the authors' tales; the dog's eyes;

the houses' walls; the cat's teeth; the house's walls; the cats' teeth;

the crocodiles' pond; the crocodile's teeth; the potion's effect; the mice's squeaks

Write a short form for these phrases.

The first one has been done for you.

the dance class for women ➔

the women's dance class

the cage of my pet bird

homes of Roman people

the sweet taste of sugar

jokes by three silly boys

Independent writing task

Information texts

In order to write about Roman food, do research on the subject first. Then use your research notes and this guide to help you write an information text.

1. My title Keep it straightforward so that the reader can recognise immediately what the text is about.	**2. The introduction** Write a short paragraph about the Romans' interest in eating well.
3. How to divide my information How many sections do you want? What will the layout of your text be?	**4. My subheadings** Use subheadings at the side above each new section: for example, 'Poor Romans' and 'Rich Romans'.

The information for each section

1. My key words Six words that you think are important to use:	**2. My illustration** Perhaps have a scene from a Roman feast in a wealthy household. Make the picture realistic.
3. The caption Make your caption a sentence that adds information to the illustration.	**4. My diagram** This simplified drawing could be of a Roman kitchen, or some of their unusual foods.

5. Labels for the diagram
Attach name labels to parts of the diagram by lines or arrows. Make the labels single words or short phrases.

Self-assessment

Read the information text you wrote. How well did you do?
Tick the features you can see in it.

Name: _____ Date: _____

- ☐ I have chosen an appropriate format.
- ☐ My layout is clear.
- ☐ I have an introduction.
- ☐ I have used subheadings.
- ☐ I have included key words.
- ☐ All illustrations and diagrams are helpful.
- ☐ My illustrations have captions.
- ☐ My diagrams have labels.

Next time, I would improve my information text by ...	Teacher's comment

I have talked to my teacher about my work on information texts.

Pupil: _____

Teacher: _____

How do muscles work?

Non-fiction: Explanation texts

Definition: *"A text about how or why something happens or works."*

Lesson objective
To recognise the writing features of an explanatory text.

Warm up activity

- Display the exemplar text, pointing out the question title. Read the text aloud.
  Ask: *What does the text achieve?* (It answers the title.)

- Challenge partners to name this type of text on individual whiteboards. Ask the children to hold up their whiteboards. Confirm *'explanation'* and discuss why. (The text explains how or why something happens or works.)

- Circle *when*.
  Ask: *What type of linking word is it?* (Time connective.) Which two words form a connective in the sentence before this? Circle *so that*, identifying the phrase as a cause and effect (causal) connective.

Features

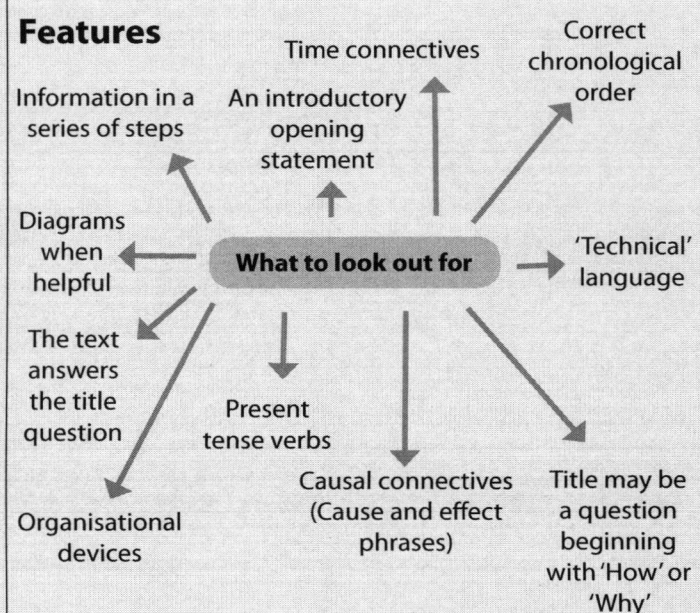

Time connectives
Correct chronological order
Information in a series of steps
An introductory opening statement
Diagrams when helpful
What to look out for
'Technical' language
The text answers the title question
Present tense verbs
Causal connectives (Cause and effect phrases)
Title may be a question beginning with 'How' or 'Why'
Organisational devices

Writing investigation
Ask the children:

- Reread the text. What helps you read and understand it? Identify four presentational features (For example, numbers).

- Compare choices with a partner. Agree on a top three and list them in order on your individual whiteboard. Hold up your board with the rest of the class. Which feature proves most important to the class? (For example: subheadings, diagrams, bold fon*t*.)

- Work with your partner to identify and list three time connectives and three cause and effect connectives.

Independent writing
Ask the children:

- This text is taken from a book about the body. Choose three or four words from the text that you would include in the book's glossary. Explain why you chose them.

- Read the final paragraph. Consider how to re-write it, changing its layout. Will you divide it into two paragraphs? Will you use presentational devices – for example, *numbers, letters or bullet points*? Are new connectives needed?

- Re-write this part of the text.

Differentiation

- More confident writers do research and add text and a diagram about another pair of muscles.
- Less confident writers do writing work with a partner.

Plenary

Use an interactive whiteboard to display the final part of the exemplar text in its original form. Invite children to say the changes they have made, and move or add text accordingly. Encourage the class to consider the clarity of the new layouts and words.

How do muscles work?

The human skeleton has more than 200 bones. Muscles are joined to the bones at joints. Muscles and joints are needed in order to allow the body to move.

Inside

Muscles contain nerve endings.
They are there so that they can respond to the brain's instructions.

When you want to move:

1. Your brain sends a message to the nerve endings.
2. One muscle gets shorter (contracts).
3. The muscle pulls on the bone.
4. At the same time, another muscle gets longer (relaxes).
5. Now the two muscles are working together to make the joint move.

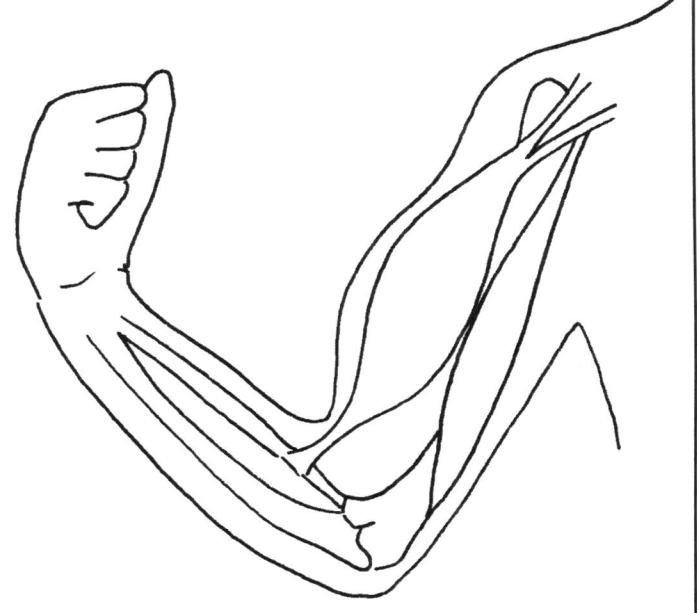

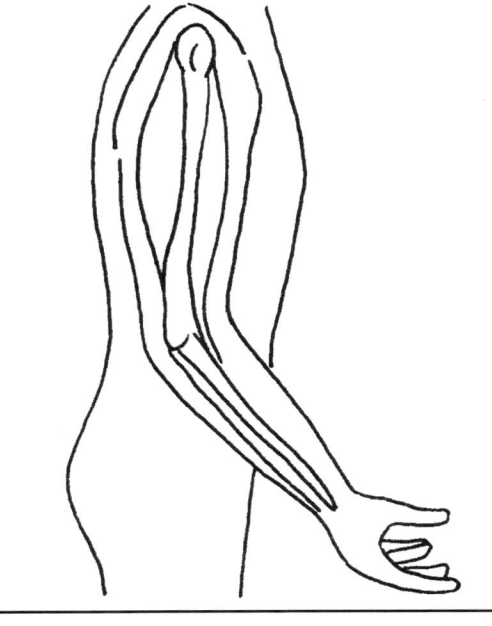

Outside

Muscles get fatter and harder when they contract.
As a result, you can often see and feel a bulge.
In order to move the joint back to where it started, the opposite happens: the relaxed muscle contracts and the other muscle relaxes.

Practice in Writing Skills 1

Causal connectives

> *Connectives* are important linking words or phrases.
> They help to hold text together.
> *Causal connectives* emphasise cause and effect.

Section A

Underline the cause and effect connective in each sentence. The first one is done for you.

You can move *because of* muscles, bones, brain and nerves.

In order to let you move, they must work together.

So that your body does not lose its shape, you have bones.

This means that you need joints where two bones meet.

Muscles have nerves endings so they can receive messages.

Muscles need exercise in case they become weak.

Muscles get weaker, unless you exercise regularly.

So therefore, sport is good for you.

As a result, you will keep moving well

Make up five sentences about yourself,

using the 'if' _____

then causal connective.

For example:

If I keep practising, then my tennis will improve.

Section B

Build sentences, in each one using a part from Box A, Box B and the connectives.

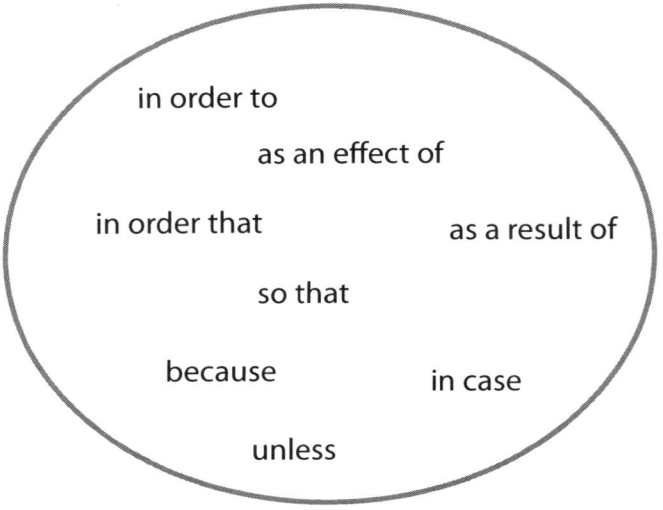

in order to

as an effect of

in order that   as a result of

so that

because   in case

unless

Box A	Box B
you need a skeleton	you catch flu
you should register with a doctor	you can bend
you will become ill	they lacked Vitamin C
you need joints	doing exercise
sailors suffered from scurvy	you need to rest
doing violent exercise	you eat well
you feel happier	you have hurt a muscle
you recover	stand up straight

Practice in Writing Skills 2

Organisational devices

A *numbered list* divides the explanation into steps and can put the steps in chronological order.
Subheadings are headings that come below the main heading. They separate a text into sections and make information easier to find.

Section A

Read this explanation of how your eyes work. It is in the wrong order. Make a numbered list out of the pieces of this explanation so it makes sense. The first one is done for you.

1	Your eyes allow you to see things. They can cope with different sources of light.
	When you are reading a book, light from a light bulb bounces off the page of the book you are looking at.
	Your brain turns the image back the right way up.
	Behind the pupil is a clear disc called a lens.
	The lens bends the light and puts an upside-down image of the page you are looking at onto the back of your eye.
	These nerve endings react to the rays of light and send the upside-down image to the brain.
	Now you can see the page of the book correctly.
	The back of your eye has special nerve endings.
	Light rays from the page pass through the pupil or black dot in the middle of your eye.

Section B

Conductor is the name for a material that allows electricity to flow through it. Metals are good conductors of electricity. However, some materials that are conductors are not metal. One example is the 'lead' that is in a pencil. This lead is really a mineral called graphite, a type of carbon. **Insulators** are materials that do not allow electricity to flow through them. Most non-metals are insulators. Rubber is one of the most effective insulators.

Read the text and plan how to divide it into four sections. On the back of this sheet, rewrite the text in the four parts with these subheadings:

What is a conductor?

Materials that are conductors

What is an insulator?

Materials that are insulators

Add another subheading and a paragraph that includes a numbered list to the text in Section B.

Independent writing task

Explanation texts → Do research about why people have Christmas trees. Then use your research notes and this guide to help you write your explanation.

1. My title
Have a question about Christmas trees beginning 'How' or 'Why'.

2. My introductory paragraph
Write a short, general introduction about what Christmas trees are and the type of tree used. Include the words *evergreen fir*.

3. My subheading
Put this at the side, for a new paragraph. For example 'Early Christmas trees'.

4. Information in a series of steps
Write about customs about 1000 years ago. List about three numbered pieces of information in correct chronological order

5. My subheading
Put a new subheading at the side. For example, 'Northern Europe' or 'Germany'.

6. Information in a series of steps
Keep to the subject of your subheading. Follow on in chronological time from the first paragraph; use a numbered list if you prefer.

7. My subheading
Put a new subheading about the custom in Britain.

8. Information in a series of steps
Follow on in chronological time from the previous paragraph.

9. When did the custom come to Britain?
Who made it popular?

10. My subheading
Put a new subheading about modern times.

11. My information in a series of steps
Follow in time from previous paragraphs. Mention homes and public places: for example, the Norwegian tree in Trafalgar Square, London. Mention artificial trees.

12. Technical language
Check that you have included correct names of people, places and things and words such as *decorations, fir, custom, celebration*.

13. Will a diagram help my explanation?

Self-assessment

Explanation texts

Read the explanation you wrote. How well did you do? Tick the features you can see in it.

Name:	Date:

- ☐ My title is a question beginning with 'How' or 'Why'.
- ☐ I start with an introductory opening statement.
- ☐ I have included 'technical' words.
- ☐ I give information in a series of steps.
- ☐ The information is in chronological order.
- ☐ My verbs are in the present tense.
- ☐ I have used time connectives.
- ☐ I have used cause and effect connectives.
- ☐ I have used organisational devices.
- ☐ I have included a helpful diagram.
- ☐ My text answers the title question.

Next time, I would improve my explanation text by ...

Teacher's comment

I have talked to my teacher about my work on explanation texts.

Pupil: _____

Teacher: _____

HELPING HANDS

Non-fiction: Persuasive texts

Definition : *"A text that aims to win the agreement of the reader."*

Lesson objective
To combine words, images and other features for particular effects.

Warm up activity

- Ask the children to imagine advertising leaflets that have been put through their letter box. Can they describe one to their partner?

- Share ideas, and describe your (imaginary) leaflet advertising a newly-opened restaurant. Use the term 'flyer'. (Text that advertises a new business or gauges interest.)

- Display and read aloud the exemplar text. Identify it as an advertisement or flyer.

Features

Organisational devices

Linguistic devices (for example, alliteration, repetition)

Language that provokes the reader's emotions

Visual impact

What to look out for

A strong concluding statement

A tone sympathetic to the reader

A question to draw the reader in

The subject targets an intended reader

Writing investigation
Ask the children:

- Consider the flyer's appearance. List two or three features that would make you want to read it. (Illustration; font variety; layout.)

- What business is being advertised? What makes the business look and sound a safe one to use? (Its name; pleasant faces; reassuring descriptions.)

- With a partner, investigate the text. Who is the intended reader? How can you tell? (The subject matter.) How does the text hold a conversation with the reader? (Questions to 'you'.) Why is this an effective device? (The reader feels more involved in the answers.)

- Identify six words that appeal to the reader's emotions by emphasising the reader's problems. How is the reader likely to react? (Get in touch with the business.) Compare and discuss your answers with your partner.

Independent writing
Ask the children:

- Study the structure and appearance of the four main sections of text. What types of sentences are used? (Questions and statements.) Which presentational and organisational features add impact? (Bold font; bullet points.)

- Think of another area of worry for the intended reader. Make up a question about it, addressing the reader directly.

- Write three statement 'answers'. Use language appealing to the reader's emotions. Emphasise the difficulties the reader presently faces and the help you can give. Follow the layout and persuasive style of previous text.

Differentiation

- More confident writers do two sections of writing.
- Less confident writers use a question. For example: Do you worry about tripping? Do you feel anxious about opening your door? Do you receive unwanted phone calls? Share the writing task with a partner.

Plenary

Put the children into groups to listen to one another's texts. Ask listeners to identify emotive words. Are they persuaded to try the businesses? As a class, investigate the end of the exemplar text. Point out reassuring information about an identification badge. Suggest that the friendly command (*So stop worrying!*) and strong finishing statement sum up the message of the whole advertisement.

HELPING HANDS

Willing workers

Caring company

Reliable helpers

Do you struggle with household jobs?
- We can move awkward furniture or heavy boxes.
- We can empty out-of-reach cupboards.
- We can deal with your rubbish and recycling.

Does shopping feel exhausting?
- We can work out a weekly list.
- We can shop with you or for you.
- We can unpack and put everything away.

Do you worry about understanding the doctor?
- We will clear up confusion over appointments.
- We will drive you to the hospital or surgery.
- We will make sure you have written follow-up advice.

Does the weather give you problems?
- We can sweep away slippery leaves.
- We can shovel through deep snow.
- We can make your dangerous drive safe with salt.

A **HELPING HAND** IS READY AND WAITING!

Just ring this number to chat about your needs: **0800 7048281**

OR

If you want us to call on you, tick the box and leave this outside. ☐

You will recognise our friendly faces from the signed HELPING HANDS identification cards. We will be pleased to show them.

So stop worrying! HELPING HANDS can do it all.

Practice in Writing Skills 1

Sentence type

There are different sentence types.
Statement: *John owns a business.*
Question: *Is he doing well?*
Command (imperative): *Talk to him about it.*

Changing the order of words in a sentence may change the sentence type.
He has worked on his own before. (statement)
Has he worked on his own before? (question)

Changing statements into commands is more complicated:
He must write everything down. (statement)
Write everything down. (command)

Section A

Identify these sentence types and write the answer between brackets. Put the missing punctuation mark at the end of the sentence. The first one is done for you.

The buildings look different. (*statement*)

What is happening in town

What are the flags for

Listen to the talk

Read the posters

A new business is opening

There is going to be a parade

Who is invited

Can animals be in it

Section B

These are statements. Change the word order and punctuation to make them into questions. The first one is done for you.

The business is doing well. ➔
Is the business doing well?

There are plenty of customers.

The dog owners have asked for advice.

They are keen that their dogs stay fit.

The walkers have answered all the questions.

Each walker will have one dog.

They can exercise each dog twice a day.

Their dog will have a snack and regular drinks.

These dogs are going to be contented.

Make up unpunctuated sentences, each written on a separate card. On the reverse of the card write the punctuated form and name the sentence type. Play a partner game, taking turns to challenge each other to punctuate a card and identify its type. Who scores better?

Practice in Writing Skills 2

Alliteration

> Alliteration occurs when closely-connected words begin with the same sound.
> These words are alliterative:
> _helping hands_; _dangerous drive_; _friendly faces_; _gnawing niggles_

Section A

Choose the alliterative word and write it in the space. The first one is done for you.

shopping _special_ (tiring ~~special~~ difficult)

list _____ (new fresh large)

snow _____ (horrid nasty sudden)

cosy _____ (conversational friendly rude)

boxes _____ (small large bulky)

furniture _____ (modern fashionable old)

Underline the two alliterative words. The first line is done for you.

with your _rubbish_ outside _recycling_

over complicated appointments confusion easy

garden dangerous your on drive

fall safe accident with salt

are remember people ready waiting

friendly will recognise our faces

Write alliterative slogans to advertise the HELPING HANDS business.

Section B

Choose the alliterative word and write it in the space.

risk _____ (break wrench jar)

flood _____ (splashes flashes soaks)

gnome _____ (plastic garden noticeable)

friend _____ (faithful honest best)

meal _____ (lunch bite mouthful)

Underline the two alliterative words. Add a third of your own.

hard jarred knocked jolted _____

steely look stare frighten _____

accident phone bone fall _____

biting wind cold blustery _____

Add an alliterative word to these.

_____ neighbour

_____ cleaning

_____ housework

_____ computer

_____ video

Independent writing task

You are starting a dog-walking service. Write an advertisement or flyer for your new business. Use this guide to help you.

1. My business name
Make the subject clear. Keep the business name short and perhaps alliterative.

2. My intended reader
Decide on the people that you want this flyer to appeal to.

3. My beginning
Have a picture of some of the dog walkers that you employ on your flyer. Use persuasive phrases or quotes about your business.

4. The planned text
How many question sentences will you use?

5. My question sentences
Write questions that will draw in your intended reader.

6. My statement answers
Use language that provokes the reader's emotions and shows your sympathy. Include repetition, alliteration and organisational devices.

7. Getting in touch
Say how to contact you. Sound friendly.

8. My conclusion
Have a persuasive finish that sums up the message of the advertisement.

9. Graphics
Aim for visual impact with pictures that suit your text. Where will you place them?

Self-assessment

Read the advertisement you wrote. How well did you do? Tick the features you can see in it.

Name: _____ Date: _____

☐ My advertisement has visual impact.
☐ I have matched my intended reader to the subject of the advertisement.
☐ I have used a question to draw the reader in.
☐ There is language that provokes the reader's emotions.
☐ My tone is sympathetic to the reader.
☐ I have used linguistic devices.
☐ I have used organisational devices.
☐ My concluding statement is effective.

Next time, I would improve my persuasive text by ...	Teacher's comment
	I have talked to my teacher about my work on persuasive texts. Pupil: _____ Teacher: _____

From a Railway Carriage

Poetry: Creating images

Definition: *"A poem that uses language to form a vivid picture for the reader."*

Lesson objective
To understand how writers use figurative and expressive language to create images and atmosphere.

Warm up activity

- While the children close their eyes, say this about your morning: *After getting up late, I swept through the house like a whirlwind*. Suggest the children draw the image of you that they 'see'. Invite partners to tell each other the impression they tried to convey. (Speed.)

- Say your words again. Ask: *Which words most influenced your picture?* (late, swept, whirlwind.)
  What was 'I' compared to? (A whirlwind.)

- Write your sentence on the whiteboard. Underline 'like'. Ask: *Why is it important?* (It forms the comparison.) Introduce the term simile, defining it as a comparison of one thing to another of a different category. Hence it creates an effective image in the reader's mind.

- Display the exemplar poem.

Features

Distinctive style or pattern

Atmosphere and mood

Effective use of language

What to look out for

Vivid mental images (imagery)

Literary devices (for example, similes)

Deliberate positioning of words and phrases

Writing investigation
Ask the children:

- Read Verse 1 with a partner. Identify a simile. What is compared to what? (Horses and cattle are compared to troops; the sights of the hill and plain are compared to rain.) Which words construct the similes? (*like; as*)

- Use partner discussion to answer these questions: *What is Verse 1's atmosphere?* (Hurried.) *What image is created of the stations?* (*Painted* makes them sound clean and cared after.) Share answers with the rest of the class.

- Read Verse 2. What image do you gain of the child (Active and alone.) Which word in the last line is particularly important? Explain your choice. (*Glimpse* reinforces the theme of speed.) Which word from the final lines of Verse 1 does glimpse support? (*Wink*.)

Independent writing
Ask the children:

- Work in a group to plan a performance of the poem. Consider rhyme, punctuation, rhythm and tempo. What tempo do the poem's words suggest? (Fast.)

- Practise by taking turns to read lines or pairs of lines aloud. Match your oral reading to the words' meaning, so that the listener 'sees' the images.

- Decide on: volume; tempo; emphasis; individual, paired or a group voice.

- Rehearse your performance. Use facial expression, gesture and body language as well as your voice.

Differentiation
- More confident writers may perform individually or in groups, adding actions and sound effects.
- Less confident writers may speak with a partner and need suggestions about how to perform.

Plenary

Let every group perform to another group or the class. Ask the audience to comment on the effectiveness of the imagery when performed. Which images do they 'see' most clearly?

From a Railway Carriage

Faster than fairies, faster than witches,
Bridges and houses, hedges and ditches;
And charging along like troops in a battle,
All through the meadows the horses and cattle;
All of the sights of the hill and the plain
Fly as thick as driving rain;
And ever again, in the wink of an eye,
Painted stations whistle by.

Here is a child who clambers and scrambles,
All by himself and gathering brambles;
Here is a tramp who stands and gazes;
And there is the green for stringing the daisies!
Here is a cart run away in the road
Lumping along with man and load;
And here is a mill, and there is a river:
Each a glimpse and gone for ever!

Robert Louis Stevenson

Practice in Writing Skills 1

Similes

A simile is a comparison between one thing and another of a different category. A simile usually uses the word 'as' or 'like'.
The train is _like_ a runner in a race.
The driver was _as_ brave as a lion.

Section A

Build similes by taking a part from each box. You can use 'like' and 'as' more than once. One simile has been made for you.

Flakes of snow fell like torn up pieces of white paper.

Sentence beginnings
Flakes of snow fell ✓
The train raced on
The driver looked as hot
The child was as busy
The sun beamed down
The trees stood upright

...to make the simile
like
as

Sentence endings
like a happy face.
a bee.
torn up pieces of white paper. ✓
a sprinter in a race.
soldiers on parade.
a blazing fire.

Section B

Compare each subject with something of a different category, but with a feature in common. Make them into similes by using 'like' or 'as'. The first one is done for you.

The painted sign was _as bright as a polished diamond._

The heavy rain fell _____

The swollen stream looked _____

The windmill's arms turned _____

The driver's eyes gleamed _____

The heavy cart moved _____

The daisies blossomed _____

The flowers were as white _____

The swaying trees _____

Create images by writing five similes of your own in descriptions of classroom objects.

Practice in Writing Skills 2

Comparative and superlative adjectives

Adjectives can have **comparative** and **superlative** forms.
The comparative form compares two alternatives.
The morning had been cold, but the night was _colder_.
The superlative form is used if you are comparing more than two.
It was the _coldest_ night for fifty years.

Longer adjectives sound too clumsy with these _er_ and _est_
endings. They use _more_ and _most_ in front of them.
A chilling wind became _more_ chilling the next day. (comparative)
It was the _most_ chilling day for sixty years. (superlative)

Section A

Write the words from the box in their correct

places in the table. One has been done for you.

tallest	hotter	newer
colder	kindest	happiest
happier	newest	hottest
oldest	safer	tiniest
safest	taller	older
tinier	kinder	coldest

Adjective	Comparative	Superlative
long	longer	longest
cold		
new		
tall		
safe		
hot		
old		
kind		
tiny		
happy		

Section B

The adjective is in bold. Write its comparative

('er' or 'more') or superlative ('est' or 'most') in

the gap. In the last two sentences, you decide

which form to use.

The spooky story seemed _____

(comparative) than before.

The film was exciting at first, and now _____

(comparative).

Matt, anxious before, was now the _____

(superlative) he had been all evening.

He needed an old cloth, the _____

(superlative) possible.

His skin felt clammy, _____

(comparative) than before.

A strange noise came from the room, the

_____ possible.

A frightened Matt, the _____

he had ever been, crept to the door.

Independent writing task

You are taking a ride in a hot-air balloon.
Write a poem describing what you see and feel.
Use this guide to help you.

1. The form of my poem Use the structure of couplets. How many pairs of lines are in a verse? How many verses? Will there be rhyme?	**2. The mood of my poem** Excited or frightened?
3. What will the tempo be? Fast or slow?	**4. My first two lines** As in the exemplar poem, divide your first line, both halves beginning with the same word.
5. Other things, places or people my poem mentions Think about what you are seeing and feeling.	**6. My similes** Have two or three. Make it clear what you are comparing to what.
7. Other vivid images Use words in carefully-chosen positions so that you create strong images for the reader.	**8. My title** Let the title say where you are.

Self-assessment

Read the poem you wrote. How well did you do?
Tick the features you can see in it.

Name: _____ Date: _____

- ☐ My poem has a distinctive style or pattern.
- ☐ There is atmosphere and mood.
- ☐ My words paint vivid mental pictures.
- ☐ I have used literary devices (for example, similes).
- ☐ I have placed words and phrases carefully.
- ☐ My poem creates images.

Next time, I would improve my image poetry by...	Teacher's comment
	I have talked to my teacher about my work on poetry that creates images.
	Pupil: _____
	Teacher: _____

Conversation

Poetry: Exploring form

Definition: *"A poem that has a style or structure to suit its subject."*

Lesson objective
To understand how form, pattern and language are used to create emphasis, humour, atmosphere or suspense.

Warm up activity
- Put the children into pairs. Can partners explain to each other what a poem is? How must it look and read? What must its form or structure be?

- Share answers, agreeing that poetry does not have to rhyme and can be in any form.

- Talk about and list unusual poetry forms that the children have experience of: tongue twisters, haiku, songs, acrostics, riddles, list poems, shape poems, alphabet and number poems, prayers.

- Display (without reading) the exemplar poem.

Features

Language with impact

Playful use of language

Phrases and words that create particular effects

Patterns ← **What to look out for** → Unusual layout

A clear style or structure

A form that suits the poem's subject

Language that provokes emotional responses

Writing investigation
Ask the children:

- Look quickly at the poem without reading it. Write down two things that you notice. Compare answers with a partner. Did you spot long and short lines or frequent question marks?

- Read the poem. Agree with your partner on a name for its form. (Question and answer.)

- Investigate the questions. What is obvious? (Most are the same single word.) Which longer question is used? (*Why don't you stop saying why?*) What is special about the last line? (It is a new single-word question.)

- Investigate the answer lines. Are they sentences? (No.) Do 'half-sentences' suit the poem's subject? Why? (A conversation is unlikely to be in complete sentences.) What is noticeable about the last answer? (Increased length.)

Independent writing
Ask the children:

- With a partner, each take a role and read the poem aloud. Notice what happens towards the end? (The person who has been giving answers now asks a question.)

- Consider your character's mood. Draw your character and hold the picture beside you as you and your partner read the roles again experimenting with voice, volume and tone. Does the person who has been giving answers get crosser? Does the questioner become louder?

- Discuss with your partner how to present the poem effectively to an audience. What performance techniques will help? What will emphasise the poem's form? Will actions and your pictures enhance the performance?

- Perform the poem for another pair of children, inviting constructive comments.

Differentiation
- More confident writers may insert 'Why?' questions and answers into the poem.
- Less confident writers may work in fours so that they speak with a partner. They will benefit from suggestions about how to perform.

Plenary

Demonstrate the use of recording software on your laptop to help poetry performance. Experiment with echo, speed changes and overdubbing effects. With the children in pairs or small groups, invite them to experiment with the software and contribute to a recording of this poem.

Conversation

I'm just going out for a moment.
Why?
To make a cup of tea.
Why?
Because I am thirsty.
Why?
Because it's hot.
Why?
Because it's summer.
Why?
Because that's when it is.
Why?
Why don't you stop saying why?
Why?
Tea-time. That's why.
High-time-you-stopped-saying-why-time.
What?

Michael Rosen

Practice in Writing Skills 1

Positive and negative statements →

A statement is a sentence that gives information.
It does not ask a question or give a command.
A positive statement states what the information is.
My house _is_ for sale.
A negative statement states what the information is not.
My house _is not_ for rent.

Section A

Sort these statements and write them in the correct boxes. One has been done for you.

Statements
Millie keeps asking questions. She does not stop.
She asks about food.   She asks about drinks.
~~Mum is not pleased.~~   Mum has an idea.
Mum does not usually behave this way.
She asks Millie a question.   Millie is surprised.
Millie will not be a pest any more.

Positive

Negative
Mum is not pleased.

Section B

Change each of these positive statements into a negative statement.

Young children are very inquisitive.

They do like to ask questions.

Adults like peace and quiet sometimes.

The questions can become a nuisance.

Parents always have the answers.

Change each of these negative statements into a positive statement.

The baby has not learned to talk.

He does not know some question words.

The question words do not prove useful.

Last week the baby did not ask lots of questions.

His Dad did not get very tired.

Practice in Writing Skills 2

Grammatical sense

> Grammatical sense means keeping *agreement* between the subject and verb in a sentence.
> The girls *is* very busy. ✘
> (Incorrect: the subject is plural, but the verb is singular.)
> The girls *are* very busy. ✓
> (Correct: the subject is plural, and the verb is plural.)
>
> *Tip: Before writing, say sentences in your head to check how they sound. After writing, read them again to check for grammatical sense.*

Section A

Circle the correct form of the verb so that each sentence has grammatical agreement.

The girls has/have a good plan.

They talks/talk to Sam.

Sam agrees/agree to help.

In the classroom their teacher is/are surprised.

There is/are always a hand up!

Someone always has/have a question.

The teacher patiently gives/give an answer.

Immediately another hand goes/go up.

There is/are no time for writing.

The children is/are too busy with questions.

The teacher is/are too busy with answers.

Section B

Find and correct 11 grammatical agreement mistakes here.

The children is really enjoying themselves. Miss Crumble decide to ignore their hands. She give no more answers. In desperation, Sam call out a question. Just then, the headmaster come in. He are shocked! Sam have broken an important rule.

"It were only a joke," explain Sam.

"Well, you gets a detention as my funny answer!" reply the headmaster.

Make up interesting sentences, using these verbs in the present tense.

Think about grammatical agreement. Afterwards, ask a partner to check your written work.

to delay, to postpone, to confuse, to reply, to query, to be, to do.

Independent writing task

Write your own question and answer conversation poem. Perhaps continue Michael Rosen's poem, with new question words. This guide will help you.

1. What my first line will be Make it an everyday statement.	**2. The structure of my poem** Who will be talking? How many lines will you have? Will your lines look very different?
3. What patterns I will have Will characters take turns to speak? Which question word will you repeat? Which words will begin the answers?	**4. How I will make the reader feel** Think about the response you want from the reader.
5. How I will provoke feelings Choose words and devices that will provoke the emotional response you want from the reader.	**6. Language that I will use playfully** These could be your pattern words or words that make the conversation sound true to life.
7. My different answer Use a statement sentence that refers to an ordinary, everyday action.	**8. My title for the poem**

Self-assessment

Read the poem you wrote. How well did you do? Tick the features you can see in it.

Name: _____	Date: _____

- ☐ My poem has a clear style or structure.
- ☐ The poem's form suits its subject.
- ☐ I have included patterns.
- ☐ I have made playful use of language.
- ☐ There are phrases and words that create particular effects.
- ☐ Some of my language provokes emotional responses.

Next time, I would improve my poetry that explores form by ...

Teacher's comment

I have talked to my teacher about my work on poetry that explores form.

Pupil: _____

Teacher: _____

GLOSSARY

adjective
A word that describes somebody or something.
The <u>wise</u> man had a <u>new</u> idea.

adverb
A word that adds meaning to a verb, an adjective, another adverb or a whole sentence.
He <u>really enjoyed</u> the game. (adverb + verb.)
It was <u>really exciting</u>. (adverb + adjective.)
The time went <u>really quickly</u>. (adverb + adverb.)
<u>Really, it was the best part of my week.</u> (adverb + sentence.)

agreement
This usually refers to grammatical agreement between nouns and verbs, when the form of a verb changes according to its subject.
This happens with the verb to be: I am/you are/ he is; and the third person singular of the present tense: I like/ she likes.

alliteration
A phrase in which adjacent or closely connected words begin with the same sound:
<u>m</u>onster <u>m</u>unches; <u>r</u>hyming <u>wr</u>iting

apostrophe (')
A punctuation mark to show:
1. contraction of words: I don't like this.
2. ownership: This is Carl's coat.

bullet point (.)
A bullet point is in bold font and is a clear way to organise an information text.

calligram
A poem in which the formation of the letters or the font selected represents an aspect of the poem's subject. A poem about fear might be written in shaky letters.

chronological writing
Writing organised to match the sequence of events.

clause
A group of words that expresses an event or a situation. She wanted a drink. It usually contains a subject (she) and a verb (wanted).

collective noun
A noun that refers to a group: crowd, herd.

colon (:)
A punctuation mark used to introduce a list or other new information relating to the first part of the sentence. I was very cold: the temperature was below freezing.

comma (,)
A punctuation mark used to help the reader by separating parts of a sentence. It may correspond to a pause in speech. In the evening, after eating, I watch television. I like films, sport and comedy.

comparative
Adjectives can have **comparative** and **superlative** forms. The comparative form of an adjective compares two alternatives. The morning had been cold, but the night was **colder**. Longer adjectives sound too clumsy with this **er** ending. They use **more** in front of them. A chilling wind became **more chilling** the next day. (comparative)

conjunction
A word used to link clauses within a sentence: It was raining <u>but</u> it was not cold.

connective
A word or phrase that links clauses or sentences and holds a text together. It can be a conjunction (e.g. but, when, because) or a connective adverb or phrase (however, therefore, as a result).

dialogue
A conversation between two parties.

direct speech
Speech that uses the speaker's original words. Inverted commas enclose the spoken words.

draft
The preliminary written form of a text.

edit
To check the content and improve the style of written work before its final form.

exclamation mark (!)
A punctuation mark used at the end of a sentence to indicate strong emotion.
Stop hurting me!

fact
Accepted, observable or demonstrable truth.

fiction
Text which is invented by a writer or speaker.

genre
The type of writing: for example adventure, legend.

imagery
The use of language to create a vivid image that appeals to the senses. Imagery is often visual.

imperative
The verb form that give orders or commands: Stop. Finish.

indirect speech
Speech that is a report of what was said, but does not use the speaker's original words.

intonation
The rise and fall of the voice.

legend
A traditional story about heroic characters, such as King Arthur. The story may be based on truth, but added to over time.

myth
An ancient, traditional story of gods or heroes which addresses a problem or concern of human existence. It may explain a fact or phenomenon.

narrative poem
A poem which tells a story.

narrative text
Text which tells of events. It may be in prose or poetry form.

noun
A word that names somebody, something or somewhere. The man took a rest at home.

onomatopoeia
Words that echo sounds associated with their meaning: clank; clatter.

paragraph
A section of a piece of writing. A new paragraph indicates a change of focus, time, place or speaker.

phrase
Two or more words that act as one unit: the broken computer, the large bag.

plural
Plural forms refer to more than one thing: trees, mice.

poetry
Text that uses features such as rhythm to convey ideas.

pronoun
A word standing in place of a noun: Sarah had a test. She was worried about it.

proper noun
The specific name of a person, place or organisation: Harry, Hyde Park.

prose
Written language that does not follow poetic or dramatic forms.

question mark (?)
A punctuation mark used at the end of an interrogative sentence.

rhyme
A rhyme occurs when words share the same stressed vowel phoneme, hence ending in the same sound: she/tea; made/lemonade

semi-colon (;)
A punctuation mark used to link two sentences closely related in meaning. I enjoyed the book; it was a pleasure to read.
A punctuation mark used to separate items in a complicated list. I bought a bag of apples; two packets of butter; a freshly-baked loaf; and some cream cakes.

sentence
A collection of words making sense on its own. It starts with a capital letter and ends with a full stop, question mark or exclamation mark. A full stop ends a sentence that makes a statement. An exclamation mark ends a sentence that expresses surprise, strong feelings or humour. A question mark ends a sentence that asks a question.

simile
A simile is an imaginative comparison. The writer creates an image in the reader's mind by comparing a subject to something else. The words *like* or *as* are usually used (e.g. the man was as strong as an ox). The girl darted from place to place like a grasshopper on the move.

singular
Singular forms refer to one thing: tree, mouse

superlative
Adjectives can have **comparative** and **superlative** forms. The superlative form is used if you are comparing more than two. It was the **coldest** night for fifty years. Longer adjectives sound too clumsy with this **est** ending. They use **most** in front of them. It was the **most chilling** wind for sixty years. (superlative)

tense
A verb form that usually indicates time.

verb
A doing, being or having word. Every sentence needs a verb. A verb can be a single word or more than one word. The boy walks home. He is walking quickly.

NOTES